Alice Childress

Twayne's United States Authors Series

Frank Day, Editor

Clemson University

TUSAS 652

ALICE CHILDRESS
© *Jerry Bauer*

Alice Childress

La Vinia Delois Jennings

The University of Tennessee at Knoxville

Twayne Publishers
An Imprint of Simon & Schuster Macmillan
New York

Prentice Hall International
London Mexico City New Delhi Singapore Sydney Toronto

PS
3505
H76
274
1995

Twayne's United States Authors Series No. 652

Alice Childress
La Vinia Delois Jennings

Twayne Publishers
An Imprint of Simon & Schuster Macmillan
866 Third Avenue
New York, New York 10022

Library of Congress Cataloging-in-Publication Data

Jennings, La Vinia Delois.
    Alice Childress / La Vinia Delois Jennings.
      p. cm.—(Twayne's United States authors series; TUSAS 652)
    Includes bibliographical references and index.
    ISBN 0-8057-3963-7
    1. Childress, Alice—Criticism and interpretation. 2. Women and literature—United States—History—20th century. 3. Afro-Americans in literature. I. Title. II. Series.
PS3505.H76Z74 1995
812'.54—dc20
                                                   95-6127
                                                     CIP

10 9 8 7 6 5 4 3 2 1

Printed in the United States of America

For my father, Robert Sydnor Jennings,
. . . In search of his request for
"seven years of knowledge . . ."
and
For my mother, Ara Belle Brown Jennings,
who like her mother stayed "to see
what the end was gonna be."

Contents

Preface: "One of the best known of unknown persons"

Alice Childress's contributions to the American stage and literature seem to be well-kept secrets. As Gayle Austin succinctly notes in "Alice Childress: Black Woman Playwright as Feminist Critic," "For southern women playwrights there was life between Lillian Hellman and Beth Henley in the 1950s and 1960s. The first play written by a black woman and professionally produced on the New York stage (in 1952) was by Alice Childress."[1] A Charleston, South Carolina, native, Childress began a formal affiliation with stagecraft in 1941 when she joined the American Negro Theatre (ANT) in Harlem, where she proceeded to do "everything there is to be done in the theatre."[2] By the decade's end she had written *Florence,* the one-act play that launched her writing career. At her death in 1994, her credits included almost a score of plays—of which more than half have been performed off Broadway or on tour—three books for adolescents, one adult novel, and an anthologized collection of fictional monologues originally serialized in Paul Robeson's *Freedom* and then in the *Baltimore Afro-American.* Her plays and novels have been praised for their assertive unsentimental treatments, strong theatrical quality, realistic dialogue, convincing characterizations, and universal appeal. Although not widely known, Childress holds the preeminent distinction of being the only African American woman whose plays have been written and professionally produced over four decades. This distinction alone positions her at the forefront of many important black theater developments of the twentieth century.

A midcentury, transitional writer, Childress did not follow in the footsteps of the male-inscribed drama that had dominated the first half of the century. When black women dramatists such as Angelina Weld Grimké, Georgia Douglas Johnson, Myrtle Smith Livingston, Alice Dunbar-Nelson, and Mary Burrill, writing between the wars, put race before gender, they conjointly with male dramatists fostered the myopic belief that truly stirring and captivating race drama was sensationalized, male-focused drama. Given priority treatment in their plays were the themes of lynching and the denigration and disenfranchisement of the black soldier. Although her plays *Florence* and *Trouble in Mind* allude to white mobs savagely murdering black men, Childress chose not to distance her art stylistically or thematically from her sex. In fact, her canon exhibits inter-textual parallels—such as the theme of the thwarted female artist and the motif of the spatial and psychological female journey—emblematic of earlier and later twentieth-century African American women writers.

Contemporary black history provided a wellspring from which Childress drew literary details, but during the initial two phases of her writing, phas-es that were concurrent with the early years of America's civil rights move-ment and the black liberationist and women's movements, Childress remained constant to her gender identity in exploring racial identity. From 1949 to the mid-1960s, interracial politics inform her work. Between these years, she consistently treats black women resisting white domination and control both inside and outside the theater. Specifically, she enacts the black woman–white woman segregated sisterhood dialectic as her first major thematic concern. As the 1960s concluded, Childress turned briefly to intraracial conflict. Probing the racial self, she indicts classism and white acculturation as artificial and destructive appropriations that undermine collective acceptance and understanding among black people.

Besides claiming centrality and visibility, the ordinary black female characters in Childress's early works reverse white and black male liter-ary stereotyping of black women. The controlling presence of Florence, Mama Whitney, Wiletta Mayer, Mildred Johnson, Julia Augustine, Tomorrow Marie Fields, and later Cora James of *A Short Walk* counter the literary image of black women as carefree, sensual, immoral repro-bates driven by the directives of their sexual instinct. Inversely, these women, driven by the directives of their rage and convictions, embark on quests for self-determination, self-identification, and self-empower-ment. A survey of Childress's work reveals the presence of strong and emergent female identities that parallel past characterizations such as Zora Neale Hurston's Janie Mae Crawford in *Their Eyes Were Watching God* (1937) and that anticipate the more recent range of full treatments by Alice Walker, Toni Morrison, and Gloria Naylor. Childress's drama functions especially as precursor to the female-centered plays of Ntozake Shangé, Vinnette Carroll, Sonia Sanchez, and Marti Charles. Preparing the way for her successors, Childress chronicled the lives of black women whose transcendence of the oppressive triad of race, class, and gender was essential and whose pronounced physical and emotional aloneness had theretofore gone virtually unrecognized and untreated. A black woman writing about the political issues of black women, Childress situ-ated the various social positions of the black woman as discrete issues within her feminist ideology.

Childress claimed partiality to the play as her most comfortable form, but it is her adolescent novel *A Hero Ain't Nothin' but a Sandwich* that remains her most recognized work. Its publication in 1973 officially initiated her third phase of writing, a period dominated by young adult fiction.' In 1978, the novel's popularity among readers of all ages soared when New World Pictures released a film version based on Childress's adaptation of her book. The novel depicts what was then a shocking portrayal of teenage drug addiction, which, like much of Childress's work, was ahead of its time in terms of social consciousness. Two other adolescent novels, *Rainbow Jordan* and *Those Other People,* have since followed. All three, written in first-person monologue style, grapple with the adolescent search for familial, peer, and communal acceptance.

Being African American, female, and a literary forerunner in exposing inequities dictated by race, class, and gender at a time when integrationist fiction was in vogue did not enhance Childress's chances for critical success. Trudier Harris suggests, "Perhaps, as with Zora Neale Hurston, Childress was overshadowed by other trends and writers during her groundbreaking years. When her *Trouble in Mind* . . . won the first Obie Award in 1956 for best original, off-Broadway play, there was more interest in integration than in the stance of affirmation of blackness that the major character takes. And Childress's play was a mere three years before the most integrationist of plays, Lorraine Hansberry's *A Raisin in the Sun* . . . , dissolved memory of others not in that vein."[3]

Childress's unwillingness to compromise her work to gain white validation or commercial viability also denied her access to theater's prestigious inner circle. Several proposed Broadway productions of her plays never materialized because she refused to relinquish control over interpretation and theme or because the work was ultimately considered commercially risky.

Despite her wide and consistent productivity in playwriting, fiction writing, directing, lecturing, and acting in stage, television, radio, and film productions, Childress's name is seldom recognized—even in connection with her own works. Scholars, critics, writers, and theater historians make only passing mention of her. Even she, in describing her literary obscurity, referred to herself as "one of the best known of unknown persons" (Harris, 68). With the recent reclamation of black women's literature and Beacon Press's 1986 reprinting of *Like One of the Family . . . Conversations from a Domestic's Life* (first published in 1956), Childress's work is just beginning to reap the respect and critical attention that it rightfully deserves.

Acknowledgments

I extend my deepest gratitude to those who assisted in the preparation of this book. I wish to thank Trudier Harris for reading chapters of this manuscript and giving her always keen and invaluable insights. I wish to thank Tamekia Clegg, for checking quotes and preparing permission requests, and Kathleen Kelly, my guru in times of crisis. Larry Doby Horton, who made possible impromptu trips to New York and Charleston, and my sister La Verne Jennings, who extended northern hospitality, deserve special mention. Many thanks to Mark Zadrozny and Frank Day for providing very sane and timely editorial assistance. I would like to thank the John C. Hodges Better English Fund of the University of Tennessee's English Department for graciously providing financial support for this project. Finally, I would like to thank Alice Childress for the rich literary legacy and courageous profile of artistic integrity she has bequeathed to us.

Chronology

1966   *Wedding Band: A Love/Hate Story in Black and White* (play).

1966–1968   Attends Radcliffe Institute for Independent Study.

1968   *The Freedom Drum,* later retitled *Young Martin Luther King, Jr.* (play).

1969   *String; Wine in the Wilderness* (plays).

1970   *Mojo* (play).

1971   Visits Russia to study Soviet life, art, and culture.

1972   *Wedding Band* performed at the Shakespeare Public Theatre, New York.

1973   *A Hero Ain't Nothin' but a Sandwich* (novel). Visits mainland China to observe the theater arts in Peking and Shanghai.

1974   Visits University of Ghana, West Africa, for summer drama festival.

1975   *When the Rattlesnake Sounds* (play).

1976   *Let's Hear It for the Queen* (play).

1977   Alice Childress Week celebrated in Charleston and Columbia, South Carolina. *Sea Island Song,* later retitled *Gullah,* performed (play).

1978   Premiere of film version of *A Hero Ain't Nothin' but a Sandwich.*

1979   *A Short Walk* (novel).

1981   *Rainbow Jordan* (novel).

1984   Artist-in-residence at the University of Massachusetts, Amherst.

1987   *Moms: A Praise Play for a Black Comedienne.*

1989   *Those Other People* (novel).

1990   Daughter Jean dies of cancer, 14 May.

1994   Childress dies of cancer in Queens, New York, 14 August.

Chapter One

"Turning against the Tide"

"I never planned to become a writer. Early writing was done almost against my will," admits Alice Childress, whose formal education ended after two years of high school, when both her mother, Florence, and her maternal grandmother, Eliza Campbell White, died. Yet by the time these two stunning losses forced her prematurely into adulthood, the foundation for her inevitable maturation into a dramatist and novelist of sizable talent had been laid. "Time, events, and Grandmother Eliza's brilliance" had taught her "to rearrange circumstances into plays, stories, novels, . . . scenarios and teleplays."[1]

Childress was born 12 October 1916 in Charleston, South Carolina. At the age of five, after her parents separated, she was sent to live in Harlem with her rather exceptional maternal grandmother. A fifth-grade education, abject poverty, and seven children who never went beyond the eighth grade did not discourage Childress's new guardian, the daughter of an former slave, from steeping herself in history, poetry, and art and becoming "a very fortunate thing that happened" in the life of her young granddaughter (Brown-Guillory 1987, 66). Grandmother Eliza had a profound influence on Childress's literary development. On many an evening, she would quiz her granddaughter on the stream of people who passed by their residence on 118th Street between Lenox and Fifth Avenues. Childress remembers her grandmother "used to sit at the window and say, 'There goes a man. What do you think he's thinking?' I'd say, 'I don't know. He's going home to his family.' She'd say, 'Well, how many children does he have?' I'd say, 'Three.' My grandmother would ask, 'Is his wife nice?' I'd say, 'No, I don't like her.' When we'd get to the end of our game, my grandmother would say to me, 'Now, write that down. That sounds like something we should keep'" (Brown-Guillory, 66). During times of adversity, her grandmother also recommended that writing be used as a method of coping. To comfort a shaken Alice after she witnessed a man gunned down in their street, Eliza White, exhorted her to "sit down, and write it down. Write."[2]

As well as activating her imagination and urging her to write, Eliza White exposed the inquisitive Childress to art, community events, and other cultures. The two constantly went on forays to public art galleries, private art showings, and neighboring communities to experience the customs, cuisines, and conversations of other ethnic groups. Her grandmother never announced the destination of these walking tours; she would simply announce, "Today we will go in this direction and ask about things" (NCTE Lecture). Once they returned home, these exploratory outings prompted recitations testing Childress's skills of observation.

The early insights Childress gained into human pain and suffering at Wednesday night testimonials at Harlem's Salem Church, where her grandmother was a member, taught her to master the art of dramatic storytelling. People in attendance, mostly women, stood before those gathered revealing troubles of a son in jail, a sick daughter, an overdue rent, or a suicide in the family. Their intensely personal confessions were often frightening, but they provided a fascinated Alice with stimulating details to store up for later use.

Other empowering females—teachers who fostered her love for reading and writing—further molded the literary artist budding inside Alice Childress. Early on she attended one year of grade school in Baltimore, but completed most of her formal education at New York's Public School 81, the Julia Ward Howe Junior High School, and Wadleigh High School. Even though her schooling subjected her to Jim Crowism, Childress recalls teachers who did make a difference. Miss Thomas, her third-grade teacher in Baltimore who threatened students with either learning to read well or remaining in her class until they were 21, made Childress a proficient reader. Her fifth-grade teacher in Harlem who took her to the library, explaining that she could draw out two books a day gratis, made her an incessant one. Literacy and open access to books gave her claim to the literary legacies of Paul Laurence Dunbar, Sean O'Casey, Guy de Maupassant, Sholom Aleichem, Shakespeare, and a host of other writers that would influence her own writing. Childress would later state that before her introduction to the library, "Writing was jotting things down." From reading and evaluating the work of other writers she learned the rules of form and structure as they applied to different genres; she then broke them in her own work to pursue her own "thought and structure patterns with failure and success" ("Candle," 114–15).

"Have-Nots in a *Have* Society"

Childress appreciatively received the good instruction that teachers provided but steadfastly resisted perpetuating the stifling trend of racial uplift literature that some suggested she imitate. They urged her to write about black "'accomplishers'—those who win prizes and honors by overcoming cruel odds" posed by "racial, physical, economic, or other handicaps." The flood of inspirational books depicting paradigm after paradigm of "the lone winner in a field of five hundred . . . or millions" induced Childress to avert these stilted and politically correct portraits of triumph that were written as much for white approval as for black encouragement. "Image-building for others to measure our [black] capability, acceptability, or human worth" was never a viable literary option for Childress. To her it seemed strangely incongruous to explain "pain to those who inflict it" and, in turn, to allow those same individuals to "claim the right to instruct us on how best to react to repression" ("Candle," 112, 113).

The result of her resistance was that she "turned against the tide" of racial uplift, concentrating on "those who come in second, or not at all—the four hundred and ninety-nine and the intricate and magnificent patterns of a loser's life." As she states, "My writing attempts to interpret the 'ordinary' because they are not ordinary. Each human is uniquely different. Like snowflakes, the human pattern is never cast twice. . . . I concentrate on portraying have-nots in a *have* society, those seldom singled out by mass media, except as source material for derogatory humor and/or condescending clinical, social analysis" ("Candle," 112).

Authentically replicating the spatial confines of those "have-not" ordinary blacks whom she respectfully calls the "genteel" or "intellectual" poor, Childress uses settings that are simple and unglamorous. Train stations, backyards, parks, tenements and the like serve as backdrops for the unfolding lives of domestics, porters, seamstresses, dancers, washerwomen, artists, and the unemployed. Her own "genteel poor" status as a young, working-class Harlemite who supported herself as a photo retoucher, insurance agent, and maid validated her claim to firsthand knowledge of the lives and lifestyles of the people that she felt repeatedly compelled to portray.

The American Negro Theatre

In 1941 Childress joined the American Negro Theatre (ANT), which had obtained space in Harlem's Schomburg Library. Although she committed herself to acting, service in all areas of stage production was required. Her various assignments included erecting sets, coaching new actors, attending to props and make-up, designing costumes, directing shows,

and serving for one year, in Frederick O'Neal's absence, as personnel
director. The only job she escaped was stage-managing. Unsalaried, the
members of the company were expected to devote four nights a week to
the theater unfailingly, even if they were not appearing in a current production. The careless violation of this attendance policy two or three
times in a row meant membership termination. Because of its grueling
schedule and rigid demands, newspaper accounts likened the ANT's
training to the rigors of a martial arts school.

Childress's first roles were as Dolly in John Silvera and Abram Hill's
comedy of manners *On Strivers' Row,* as Polly Ann in Theodore Browne's
folk drama *Natural Man,* and as Blanche in the original American version of Philip Yordan's Polish play *Anna Lucasta,* which Abram Hill suggested be adapted to portray a black family. A runaway success, *Anna
Lucasta* went to Broadway. Its 30 August 1944 premiere at the
Mansfield Theatre extended to 957 performances and earned Childress a
Tony Award nomination. Hilda Simms, Earle Hyman, Canada Lee, Ossie
Davis, Ruby Dee, Sidney Poitier, and other black performers who
appeared in the off-Broadway and Broadway productions went on to
national and international fame.

An 11-year apprenticeship with the ANT instilled theater discipline
in Childress, but left her unfulfilled artistically. The productions paid
much more attention to issues significant to black men than to black
women. Her powerlessness to dismantle stock female roles and to construct the type of roles she wanted to see performed became the primary motive in her decision to become a playwright. The observation
that there was "almost as much injustice in the theatre as there is in
the rest of the land"[3] solidified her dislike for the "business" of acting
and auditioning. Her own entanglement in a complexion Catch-22—
she was considered too light to cast in black roles while her race ruled
out white parts—intensified her impatience with the limits of stock
casting. After the Tony nomination for her role in *Anna Lucasta,* "radio
and television work followed," states Childress, "but racism, a double
blacklisting system, and a feeling of being somewhat alone in my ideas
caused me to know I could more freely express myself as a writer"
("Candle," 115).

A neophyte dramatist anxious to try her hand at portraying female
characters, Childress wrote her first play, *Florence* literally overnight. Her
composition, written in one act in 1949, directly challenged the persist-
ing assumption that the only important race drama was sensationalized,
male-inscribed drama. Her goal was "to settle an argument with fellow

actors (Sidney Poitier among others) who said that, in a play about Negroes and whites, only a 'life and death thing' like lynching is interesting on stage."[4]

Mama Whitney, the ordinary, working-class black protagonist, inaugurated Childress's depiction of the "genteel" poor. On her way by train to retrieve her daughter Florence from a failing New York theater career, Mama changes her mind when, through an encounter with a condescending white woman, she realizes that she cannot rely on white liberal women to empower her daughter. A serious black drama coming at the end of a decade that had begun with black theater largely relegated to vaudeville comedies and musicals, *Florence* made a small but significant dent in reconceptualizing the potential of black theater. Its appearance anticipated the revolutionary theater of protest, or accusation, developed in the 1960s by dramatists such as Sonia Sanchez and LeRoi Jones (Imamu Amiri Baraka). It also foreshadowed the later female-centered drama of Vinnette Carroll and Ntozake Shange.

Although the reason for the delay is uncertain, Childress did not immediately follow up the production of *Florence* with another drama focusing on the black female. Her next project, an adaptation from print to stage, led to the successful production of *Just a Little Simple* by the Committee for the Negro in the Arts (CNA) in 1950. Langston Hughes's racially edged satire *Simple Speaks His Mind,* serialized conversations in the *Chicago Defender* that were anthologized in a book of the same title earlier in the year, lent itself well to restructuring as a dramatic musical revue. It opened in September at the Club Baron Theatre on Lenox Avenue for a two month-run, playing to a total audience of 8,000. The play featured Kenneth Mannigault as Jesse B. Semple, a "simple" man of the people and the master-of-ceremonies in a Harlem variety show. Adding to the evening's enjoyment was a revival of *Florence. Just a Little Simple* drew laudatory reviews and speculation about a Broadway opening, but the producers maintained that the uptown show was intended to advance the concept of a Negro theater, not achieve billing on Broadway.

Childress's personal encounters with racism in America and her heightened sensitivity to apartheid in South Africa inspired her next stage production. *Gold through the Trees* premiered on 7 April 1952, the day of black South Africa's civil disobedience protest of the tricentennial of the South African Boers. It depicted blacks on both continents struggling to free themselves from racial oppression. The historical, musical revue in eight scenes ran through 19 May at the Club Baron. Clarice

Taylor, Vinnie Burroughs, Hilda Haynes, Helen Martin, and Childress herself performed in the production, which was the first play by a black woman to be professionally produced on the American stage. The earlier success of *Just a Little Simple* had spurred Childress to negotiate the first off-Broadway union contracts that recognized the Actors Equity Association and the Harlem Stage Hand Local.

Gold through the Trees attracted the first review of an original work by Childress. Lorraine Hansberry, her coworker at Paul Robeson's newspaper *Freedom,* critiqued the production, signing only her initials to the piece.

Her two stage successes in the five years following *Florence* encouraged Childress to renew her writing of black female drama. Now a veteran at stagecraft, Childress began a direct attack on the dramatic arts' failure to present the ordinary black American woman's experiences void of stereotypes. In contrast to the falsely romantic stock figures of black women in popular literature, Childress created the aging black female protagonists imbued with the spiritual essence of her grandmother Eliza White. Her characters may be "impoverished and lacking formal education but . . . [their] love of art and learning—along with a fierce personal pride and independence—makes them admirable."[5] By and large, her black female characters strive to erase the misnomer of matriarch often ascribed to black women and to inscribe their own definitions of self. They begin to see their missions as, simultaneously, claiming artistic control, mediating their anger constructively, and exposing white women's and black men's culpability in perpetuating racist and sexist oppression.

The thwarting of the black theater artist that was treated in absentia in *Florence*—the title character never appears in the play—literally took center stage in *Trouble in Mind,* Childress's first full-length drama. A play within a play, the comedy metadrama depicts the frustration that black actors and actresses experience in mainstream white theater because only limited and demeaning parts are made available to them. Demanding self-definition, Childress, like the play's main character, Wiletta Mayer, stressed that internal agitation and opposition to invalid, other-imposed images of black men and women were essential to reclaiming the image of blacks inside and outside the theater. Black actors and actresses, Childress believed, must not tolerate or perform dramas riddled with shuffling darky figures and handkerchief-head mammies. She based Wiletta's spiritedness on Georgia Burke, a cast member of *Anna Lucasta*. Burke would go along with most requests, but some days she would announce she was tired of accommodating others.

Childress and Clarice Taylor, who appeared as Wiletta, directed the first production of *Trouble in Mind* in 1955, which ran for 91 performances. Because their producer threatened to cancel the production if it did not end happily, their three-act play concluded with Wiletta successfully negotiating a realistic presentation of blacks with the white director of the outer play. Shortly thereafter, Childress, hating herself for giving in and making the change, reinstated the original ending; thus the 1957 version of the play, published in Lindsay Patterson's *Black Theatre,* compressed into two acts, ends with the anticipation of Wiletta's dismissal from the cast.

It is ironic that the same white artistic control the play repudiates worked to prevent its appearance on Broadway. *Trouble in Mind* opened on 4 November 1955 at the Greenwich Mews Theatre of the Village Presbyterian Church and Brotherhood Synagogue at 141 West 13th Street in Greenwich Village. It went on to win the *Village Voice* Obie Award for the best off-Broadway play of the 1955–56 season. The play then drew Broadway speculation when Edward Eliscu optioned it for production. But after two years of negotiations in which demands for script changes and disputes over theme and interpretation ensued, it was abandoned as a poor commercial risk.

"Here's Mildred"

Blacks who read Childress's weekly column "Here's Mildred" in the *Baltimore Afro-American* cheered on the feisty New York maid who said and did, particularly in response to the racism of the white women who hired her for day work, what they in real life desired to say and do. The persona of Mildred turned against the traditional tide of self-effacing domestics of past literature, and her outspokenness "had little of the God-fearing, long-suffering tolerance that would characterize Lorraine Hansberry's Mama Lena Younger a few years later in *A Raisin in the Sun.*"[6]

Drawing from the black oral tradition of signification, especially the creation of a mythical, heroic self, Mildred uses indignation and a take-charge approach against the indignities that assail her during the execution of her work. Her special talent for thoroughly engaging her audience hinges on her combining satire and humor "with a political vengeance" to combat racial prejudice.[7] Picking up where Wiletta in *Trouble in Mind* left off, Mildred is unwilling to be silenced or to compromise her dignity for pay.

Earning Childress $25 per submission, "Here's Mildred" bore the influential markings of Hughes's serialization of Jesse B. Semple in the *Chicago Defender* and Childress's own successful dramatization of the Semple character in 1950. "Conversation from Life," sketches of Mildred that ran briefly in Paul Robeson's *Freedom* prior to being picked up by the Baltimore newspaper, culminated in *Like One of the Family . . . Conversations from a Domestic's Life,* published in 1956.

Childress based many of Mildred's exploits on the day-work experiences of her Aunt Lorraine and on her own domestic assignments during the years she apprenticed with the ANT and had to make financial ends meet. Being asked to supply medical documentation to prove that she was disease-free and observing that one of her employers was unable to put down her purse in her own home for fear that Childress would steal its contents were the types of galling incidents she endured from time to time. Childress relieved the stress of one such situation by abruptly terminating her employment, throwing a set of keys at the head of her white female employer as she departed.

Through Mildred, Childress sought to explode many of the stereotypes associated with black women who daily worked in the homes of whites. The 62 conversations are testaments to the resilience of black domestics, who did much backbreaking work for their own families and the families of others but who received little respect, little pay, and little acknowledgment for their service. "In Mildred," writes Trudier Harris in her introduction to a 1986 reprint of *Like One of the Family,* "Childress seldom romanticizes the domestic worker, but she does suggest that that position was not ultimately so negating that it does not warrant celebration in the literature. *Like One of the Family* celebrates the image of black women most common to their history and suggests that they are no less dignified for having spent time on their knees. Mildred scrubs and soars. In both postures lies the complexity of black women" (xxxiii).

Rebel Spirits

For Childress, composing *Wedding Band: A Love/Hate Story in Black and White,* the play in which she explores miscegenation, was "like being possessed by rebel spirits." While she was trying to write something else, the characters kept "demanding attention," calling her from "hidden, unexpected places." The writing, "instead of a joyous experience became a trial, a rough journey through reams of paper." The play, composed and first performed in 1966, Childress felt, "somehow seemed to be answering back all the stage and screen stories about rich, white landowners and their 'octoroon' mistresses."[8] She decided that her depiction would not be a modern-day construction of the old plantation formula of the white colonel's exploitation. Nor would she mimic the pattern of the colonel's black sweetheart "never [seeming] to know any men of her own race" except "slack-kneed objects of pity."[9] It had not been her wish "to beat the drum for an interracial couple," she said, but rather to indict "anti-woman" laws, laws prohibiting marriage and divorce framed with the intent of denying women control over their lives and bodies (Betsko and Koenig, 63).

Childress based her play on a true story told to her by her mother Florence and grandmother Eliza. A "black woman named Miss Julia, who lived across the street from [them] in South Carolina and who 'kept company' with a white butcher" supplied the outlines for the lives of Julia Augustine and her white common-law husband, Herman. Because South Carolina law decreed interracial marriage illegal, the two could not live together as man and wife. Childress made Julia's lover in the play a baker "because she thought it would be more palatable for the audience than butchering" (Betsko and Koenig, 64). She also did not give him a last name, seeing it as pointless since Julia could not have it.

Ignoring the fact that this situation often occurred in real life, black critics scorned Childress's choice of subject—interracial love—arguing that "Miss Julia should not have wanted to marry a white man" (65). John O. Killens viewed the drama as a "deviation" from Childress's other writings, which had "a total and timely relevance to the Black experience in the U.S. of A. . . . It was difficult," he posits, "to empathize or identify with the heroine's struggle for her relationship with the white man, symbolically the enemy incarnate of Black hopes and aspirations" (131).

White critics of *Wedding Band* complained that the interracial couple should have just fled north to marriage and a better life, leaving behind the South and the baker's mother and sister, who were dependent on him as their sole support. Defending her choice of having the couple remain in a "city by the sea . . . South Carolina, U.S.A.,"[10] Childress insisted that fleeing from familial responsibility is "a very hard thing for poor people to do. It's easier for wealthy people. They can leave *and* send money home to their dependents," but "to walk away from family and debts is almost unheard of in poor communities" (Betsko and Koenig, 64).

The Alice Childress–Clarice Taylor production performed at the University of Michigan at Ann Arbor in December 1966 featured Ruby Dee, Abbey Lincoln, Taylor, and Moses Gunn. When Joseph Papp with

Bernard Gersten produced the play at New York's Shakespeare Public Theatre on 26 November 1972, Ruby Dee appeared once again as Julia, with James Broderick appearing opposite her as Herman. Childress began as director of the production but was relieved of her position before the premiere—on the third night of standing-ovation previews—with Papp taking over. The Papp production, retaining much of Childress's original direction, drew similar criticism from both racial quarters, but on the whole opened to good reviews. Only a Chicago production, which appeared in 1971, held widespread black appeal, selling out its entire six-week run to standing-room-only audiences.

Prior to *Wedding Band*'s debut, Broadway options hovered dimly in the shadows; but as in the cases of *Just a Little Simple* and *Trouble in Mind,* a production never materialized. Conceding race and gender bias, Joseph Papp admitted that the play would have gone to Broadway if it had been less Julia's play and more Herman's. ABC television nationally aired the Public Theatre production of *Wedding Band* as a two-hour prime-time special in 1973, but because of its taboo interracial theme, eight affiliates refused to broadcast it. Others aired it only after midnight.

For Blacks about Blacks

The unfolding politics of black liberation and power of the 1960s channeled Childress's dramatic attention inward to the examination of the racial self. When Tillie Olsen recommended her for an appointment as playwright and scholar to the Radcliffe Institute (now the Mary Ingraham Bunting Institute) for Independent Study from 1966 to 1968, she took the opportunity to finish some of the dramatic projects that would appear on stage at the conclusion of the 1960s. Working with other appointees who held doctorates, Childress was awarded a graduate medal for the writing she produced while at Radcliffe. Lillian Hellman, one of the program's judges, may have evaluated her work.

In 1968, Childress staged *The Freedom Drum,* which she later retitled *Young Martin Luther King, Jr.,* a historical play in tribute to the slain civil rights leader and apostle of nonviolence. It was touring the country when *Wine in the Wilderness, String,* and *Mojo, A Black Love Story,* three one-act plays that Childress staged in quick succession, appeared between 1969 and 1970. Written for blacks about blacks, these three plays responded to the intraracial classism and sexism growing out of the black liberationist movement. Each presents from different viewpoints the social dysfunction that white acculturation and class conditioning cause when bourgeois blacks fail to respect poorer black men and women as their social and political equals.

Underwritten by the Ford Foundation, *Wine in the Wilderness* was aired by WGBH in Boston on 4 March 1969 as the first production in the public television station's series *On Being Black.* The state of Alabama refused to carry the broadcast. In the same month, *String* was presented by New York's Negro Ensemble Company on March 25 at St. Mark's Playhouse, under the direction of Edmund Cambridge. A loose adaptation of Guy de Maupassant's tale "The Piece of String," the production featured Esther Rolle, Clarice Taylor, Arthur French, Frances Foster, and Julius W. Harris. In 1979, PBS aired a production of the play. Roger Furman directed the November 1970 production of *Mojo,* performed by the New Heritage Theatre in Harlem, which starred Emett Wallace and Jean Taylor.

Writing for Young Adults

Childress's sheltered journey toward adulthood in the 1930s differed radically from the teen years of the characters depicted in her adolescent fiction. "On our block there was prostitution," Childress recalls, "but we were so damned blind until even the prostitutes were called 'Miss' Margaret or 'Miss' Beatrice or whatever. And they did not beckon to men until our backs were turned, most of the time. Heroin was not yet King of the Ghetto and a boy would not dream of killing his grandmother or hurting his mama or her friends in order to pour cooked opium dust through a hole in his arm" (Betsko and Koenig, 64).

Childress, who had reared a teenage daughter—Jean—between the late 1940s and early 1950s, was distressed by children's increasing exposure to experiences beyond their years in the 1960s and 1970s. She dismayingly noticed that works confronting social and political issues honestly and in depth were frequently derided and pushed to the margins because of their "controversial nature," while "murder as a form of casual amusement" and "the blatant sexual exploitation of children" were "presented as art forms" ("Candle," 113).

An unexpected induction into the young adult publishing world marked a major literary turning point for Alice Childress. Far from having to fight and struggle to get a work produced, as she had in the theater, Childress was invited—almost by accident—to write her first young adult novel. Ferdinand Monjo, the now late editor and noted children's author, encouraged her to write *A Hero Ain't Nothin' but a Sandwich* after noticing her interest in the drug theme in earlier works.

Childress had also previously addressed the concerns of young people. In *The World on a Hill* (1968), a one-act play, a wealthy white woman and a poor West Indian youth bridge boundaries of age, race, class, and gender, and in a scene from *The African Garden* (1971), also a play, Childress depicts a black adolescent's desperate need for adult acknowledgment of his personhood. But *Hero* was her first effort to write specifically for young adults.

Because she had been reared by a caring adult other than her mother, Childress felt it important to emphasize adults' responsibility in rearing children other than their own. She also wanted to allay the basic fears and anxieties common to all teens. Reflecting on her own childhood, she found baffling adults who looked at her and other children and commented on how "wonderful" it was to be young, since they didn't have to worry about anything. Yet all the while she knew that she, like many other children, had "a worry program" (NCTE Lecture).

In her adolescent fiction Childress especially wanted to address socially current topics that most threatened young adult survival. But topical openness on issues most absorbing to teens—drugs, teen pregnancy, racism, homosexuality, and divorce—led Childress into controversy. Deemed offensive because of its indecent (sexual) content, profane language, and identification as a "drug" book, *A Hero Ain't Nothin' but a Sandwich,* along with nine other books, was banned from the Island Trees School library in New York in 1976.[11] The censorship case, *Board of Education, Island Trees Union Free School District v. Pico* (1982), wended its way to the U.S. Supreme Court, the first of its type to be heard by the Court. *A Hero Ain't Nothin' but a Sandwich* was also the first book banned from a Savannah, Georgia, school library since the 1950s banning of J. D. Salinger's *The Catcher in the Rye* (1945), perhaps the singularly most controversial American adolescent novel of all time.

An avid practitioner of character over plot, Childress relied heavily on her training as a playwright in the construction of a loose narrative style. When composing her adolescent fiction, Childress visualized each of the chapters as scenes, charting her characters' movements by actually walking about and acting out all of their parts. Playwrights, she testifies, are "specialists in dialogue, situation and conflict; and they must make it all happen within a limited time and space." Consequently, descriptive writing was particularly challenging to her. "With plays, after we've described the set," Childress explains, "we're free of that. We don't have to describe the sun rising or the sound of rain. Someone else brings lighting, set, costumes and sound to life for us."

Learning to "lean on theater instead of breaking with it," Childress practiced an economy of description in her adolescent and adult fiction (Betsko and Koenig, 67). Characters deliver the primary narrations of their stories in a dramatic, first-person monologue style that minimizes or totally eliminates authorial or omniscient narrational intrusions. She was always pleased when her fiction was noted for its dramatic quality, since the compliment implies that her books are highly visual.

Childress also wrote two plays for young people: *When the Rattlesnake Sounds* (1975) and *Let's Hear It for the Queen* (1976). Mindful of the positive role heroic figures from the past can play in teaching lessons of moral consciousness and commitment to today's youth, Childress features the abolitionist Harriet Tubman and the theme of bravery in the midst of fear in her historically instructive *When the Rattlesnake Sounds*. *Let's Hear It for the Queen* (1976), a play for preadolescent performance that she wrote for her granddaughter, Marilyn Alice Lee, in celebration of her eighth birthday, disrupts sexist typecasting and addresses in a simplified manner the theme of crime and punishment.

Gullah

Because much of Childress's work is set in and influenced by Harlem and her native Charleston, it seems inappropriate, if not impossible, to classify her definitively as a northern or a southern writer. Throughout her life, she did not break ties or faith with her state of birth, and South Carolina proudly claims her as its native daughter. To commemorate "Alice Childress Week," in 1977 the South Carolina Commission on the Arts requested that she write an original, hour-long play that could be performed at school assemblies across the state between 10 October and 17 December. Childress submitted *Gullah,* a collaboration with her husband, musician Nathan Woodard, who composed original scores for the play. *Gullah* celebrated the Africanisms of the black people of the islands off the South Carolina coast, whose lyrical language evolved from many African tongues, mixed with English and German. Childress's personal connection to the Gullah people stemmed from her stepfather, a native of Edisto, one of the islands. When he died and she met his relatives, she was much impressed with the remarkable sound of the unintelligible language they spoke.

"Using the convention of the funeral procession stopping at the gates of the cemetery to wait for permission to enter from the Gate Spirit, who in this case, says 'no,'" Childress called the drama "a folk story as the islanders would tell it."[12] Set on Johns Island, the plot centers around a poor man who becomes rich and the disastrous effect his newfound wealth has on him. Leonard Peters directed the musical production, and its cast of seven included Stephen Bordner, Guy Davis, Thelathia Barnes, Deborah Winters, Denise Gray, Regina DeLossantos, and Learie Jones.

For the South Carolina production, *Sea Island Song* replaced the original title of the play, since the commission felt the word "Gullah" conjured up negative images of backward country folk. Sensing that the new title sounded misleadingly Hawaiian, Childress reverted to the original when the University of Massachusetts at Amherst staged a production in the spring of 1984.

A Short Walk

Within the covers of *A Short Walk* (1979), one can see Childress reaping the benefits of Eliza White's encouragement to write down bits and pieces of her daily life. Her early autobiographical jottings appear thinly veiled throughout the novel's sweeping fictionalized survey of the minstrel show era, the Jazz Age, the Garvey movement, and the "get by" lives of blacks during the Great Depression.

At the novel's beginning, 15-year-old Murdell Johnson's conception of Cora James roughly echoes the conception story of Childress's grandmother Eliza. Hired as a live-in maid for a white family, Murdell has an affair with her employers' son, whom they send away once they discover that she is pregnant with his child. Similarly, Childress's great grandmother Ani (or Annie) at emancipation was abandoned at the age of 12 on the streets of Charleston by her former slavemaster. Befriended by Anna Campbell, a white woman who extended her a home, Ani became pregnant by her benefactress's son, a merchant seaman, who sailed away never to return after she became pregnant with his child.

Like Cora's gradual immersion into the dramatic arts during her primary school years, Childress's abiding love for Shakespearean drama grew as her skills of reading and recitation sharpened. Childress's first theatrical experience was that of hearing actress Laura Bowman recite from the Bard's canon. The first role she recalls performing, paralleling Cora's first, is that of Titania in *A Midsummer Night's Dream*. Childress's appreciation of Shakespeare continued to flourish during her association with the ANT. The numerous responsibilities the company exacted of her did not restrict her association with a Harlem troupe that performed only Shakespearean plays.

One of the many innovative approaches Childress's grandmother used to handle crises is tucked into a scene in which Cora James turns a stalker into a gentleman by enlisting him to escort her and her daughter Delta home from a Wednesday night testimonial meeting. The harrowing episode, which actually happened to Childress and her grandmother as they left a church gathering, is recorded almost identically to the real-life incident.

A marginal success, *A Short Walk* seems to have never fully targeted its intended readership. Coming on the heels of Childress's successful children's fiction, the adult novel was often mistaken as junior fiction. Another problem was the negative review the book drew from Alice Walker in *Ms.* magazine. "[T]he novel disappoints," because of its "forced folksiness throughout that makes much of what is said between characters unbelievable." Moreover, Walker maintained, it lacks "passion (though not anger) . . . as well as, in some instances, originality."[13] Cora's marriage to an older man of property calls to mind Janie Mae Crawford's in Hurston's *Their Eyes Were Watching God* (1937), Walker said, while Cora's fight to raise a child in Harlem smacks of Lutie Johnson in Ann Petry's *The Street* (1946). Other reviewers were more favorable, with one praising the book as unpredictably "remarkable" and "as a veritable celebration of the black community's use of language . . . rich, both in imagery and adroitly used proverbs."[14] Walker's views, however, carried the day.

"Moms": Many Childress Women in One

When *Moms, A Praise Play for a Black Comedienne,* appeared at the Hudson Guild Theater in February of 1987, the flesh-and-blood life of Loretta Mary Aiken (pseudonymously Jackie "Moms" Mabley) seemed coincidentally but appropriately to have embodied almost all of the aging (and some of the young) ordinary black female characters that Childress had spent the last four decades of her life fictively creating. As a young mother sacrificing the personal rearing of her children to pursue a stage career, Mabley is Florence. As a black woman starting out in the racist minstrel show era, she is Cora James. As a stand-up comic capable of mixing equal parts humor and satire with political vengeance, she is Mildred Johnson. As the black female artist who preferred to create and perform her own roles of blackness over acting out those as servants in white operas, she is Wiletta Mayer. And as the frumpy "messed up chick" who defied social appearance to assert a dignified reality, she is Tomorrow Marie Fields.

Even more coincidental is the professional and political resemblance that Mabley, the comedienne, bears to Childress, the playwright and author. Marginalized as performers by virtue of their femaleness and blackness, both acquired a goodly measure of self-discipline that enabled them to endure. And both in their endurance went against the social tide of what black women were expected to be, do, think, and say. The *New York Times* said of *Moms* that in Mabley's "attacks on racism and sexism, we can see the soul of a social commentator,"[15] and the same could be said of Alice Childress. It is in the role of social commentator and critic that Childress rose to her artistic best.

Chapter Two

"Ain't You Mad?": Women, Anger, and Interracial Conflict

As America's depressed economy and theater revived concurrently during World War II, the staged black productions throughout the 1940s—Childress's first decade of work in the theater—composed a medley of the dramatic types of the preceding 40 years. As Doris Abramson notes, the "inevitable musical"—*Cabin in the Sky* (1940) and *Carmen Jones* (1943)—and the "wartime vaudeville"—*Harlem Cavalcade* (1942) and *Blue Holiday* (1945)—occupied the Broadway stage during the first half of the decade (Abramson, 95).

As in the 1920s and 1930s, the serious dramas of only a few black playwrights gained Broadway status. Two of the most notable, both social protest plays, were *Native Son* (1941), Richard Wright's dramatic coadaptation with Paul Green of his critically acclaimed deterministic novel, published in 1940, and *Our Lan'* (1947), Theodore Ward's historical play about the Reconstruction era. Reminiscent of the "black" drama of Eugene O'Neill, Paul Green, and Marc Connelly, *Deep Are the Roots* (1945) by Arnaud d'Usseau and James Gow was the period's most successful Broadway play written by whites to address seriously the issue of race.

Off Broadway, the American Negro Theatre, which Childress joined in 1941, brought to the stage the plays of talented black playwrights. These included *On Strivers' Row* (1940), John Silvera and Abram Hill's treatment of the black bourgeoisie, and *Natural Man* (1941), Theodore Browne's adaptation of the legend of steel-driving John Henry. A black adaptation of Philip Yordan's Polish drama *Anna Lucasta* (1944) was taken to Broadway and became the ANT's most successful production.

Though the ANT staged many fine productions and taught her much about acting and dramaturgy, Childress, then in her mid-20s, found herself increasingly aware that her gender and racial concerns were neither featured nor reflected in the productions on which she worked. A challenge to prove that male-dominated plots and issues did not define the order of African American life or of the American black stage compelled her to create a dramatic world in her own image.

The 1950s, considered the decade of emergence for the black playwright, was primed for Childress's debut as a dramatist. Along with William Branch's *A Medal for Willie* (1951) and *In Splendid Error* (1954), Louis Peterson's *Take a Giant Step* (1953), Loften Mitchell's *A Land beyond the River* (1957), and Lorraine Hansberry's *A Raisin in the Sun* (1959), Childress initiated her black female-centered playwriting with *Florence* (1949), a one-act drama, followed with *Trouble in Mind* (1955), a play in three acts. Though Childress wrote other plays during her first 20 years as a dramatist, *Wedding Band: A Love/Hate Story in Black and White* (1966) concludes the first major phase of her playwriting and production.

Situated in the midst of these plays, her collection of 62 short monologues, *Like One of the Family . . . Conversations From a Domestic's Life* (1956), seems typologically odd. But the vibrant, dramatic first-person delivery of the conversations renders them as theatrical as any of the plays in Childress's canon. Connected most visibly by subtle and direct displays of black female anger, each of the four works deals with the psychological journey that black women must take, particularly those of suppressed artistic sensibilities, to address and redress interracial conflict.

Collectively, the major works of Childress's first phase of writing are dramas of revolution, protest, or accusation, generally centering on violent verbal and physical confrontation between blacks and whites. With their appearance between 1949 and 1968, Childress's plays prefigure the revolutionary drama of Sonia Sanchez, Barbara Molette, Martie Charles, Ntozake Shange, LeRoi Jones (Imamu Amiri Baraka), and Ed Bullins in the mid-1960s and 1970s.

Segregated Sisterhood and Anger

In most critical discussions of the first phase of Alice Childress's writing career, the interracial conflicts in her works overshadow and displace the gender conflicts. As gendered texts, the scripts of *Florence, Trouble in Mind,* and *Wedding Band* and the dramatic monologues that make up *Like One of the Family . . . Conversations from a Domestic's Life* delineate through characterization, plot, and theme sociopsychological complexities uniquely female in insight and experience. The black female protagonists in these works exercise their right to self-actualization, to resist the conventions of motherhood, and to renounce other-imposed images and definitions of themselves. As evolving black women, they demand public and private equality in the arts, in the workplace, and in love.

Politically aware of the racial dissonance among women, Childress deliberately calls forth the black woman–white woman segregated sisterhood dialectic as her first frontier for dramatic exploration. In doing so, she depicts women confronting women about the roles, choices, differences, hypocrisies, and racism of women. Within her depictions, black female characters use anger and defiance as means of exorcising the psychic hostility that America's history of white racism, as unseen signifier, breeds between white and black, between noncolored women and women of color.[1]

Childress's fictional portraits illustrate the real-life fact that white women have on occasion acknowledged the tensions that have plagued their relationships with black women from slavery through the racially divided women's movements of the late nineteenth- and twentieth-centuries. But they also stress that white women have rarely dealt effectively with the more pressing issues behind those tensions.[2] Childress's noncolored women characters, especially those claiming bourgeois status, deny their culpability in perpetuating a white, patriarchal, racist ideology and fail to redress their own racist treatments of black women. Furthermore, they feel justified in responding to ensuing black female rage with reciprocal anger.

Foremost, the anger in Childress's work does not exist solely for the sake of anger. Her treatment of anger converts it from a disruptive, useless principle into a constructive liberating force. Anger becomes one of the major catalysts in Childress's black women enabling growth, vision, voice, direction, empowerment, and change. Breaking their racialized code of silence, these women vocalize racially provoked anger and access verbal and rhetorical gestures of triumph and transcendence over white female disempowerment.

For Childress's black female characters, "anger," as Carol Tavris's study of the emotion states, "is as much a political matter as a biological one. The decision to get angry has powerful consequences" and has "an emphatic message: *Pay attention to me. I don't like what you are doing. Restore my pride. You're in my way. Danger. Give me justice.*"[3] In *Trouble in Mind,* Wiletta Mayer turns her suppressed rage against the white patriarchy of the theater and steadfastly resists perpetuating its false formulations of black identity. *Florence, Wedding Band,* and *Like One of the Family* pit black women directly against white women who, placing color over sisterhood, replicate the racist behavior and exclusionary practices of white patriarchy. As further amplification of the white woman's appropriation of the exclusionary practices of white men and her complicity in the perpetuation of a segregated sisterhood, Childress illustrates how white women in positions of power fail to make a difference with regard to gender because of racial bias.

Retaliating with anger, Mama Whitney in *Florence* and Julia Augustine in *Wedding Band* unleash pent-up hostilities at racist upper- and lower-middle-class white women that lead to the alterations of their own psychic bases. Both realize that they are responsible not for altering the psyches of their female oppressors but for the condition of their own. Conversely, In *Like One of the Family,* Mildred Johnson channels her undercurrent of indignation and anger into actions and words that raise the consciousness and diffuse the racist behavior of the white women who hire her.

Florence

A cursory structural and thematic examination of *Florence,* the one-act play Childress wrote in 1949 for the American Negro Theatre,[4] may suggest that the work is little more than a slight, static drama depicting southern racism under institutionalized Jim Crowism. Moreover, the observation that the play is Childress's first attempt at professional play-writing, as well as an overnight creation, might further advance the simple assessment that it is not as well-structured as her later drama. A deeper analysis, however, reveals a subtly powerful, well-crafted play. Indeed, *Florence* serves as a signature or set piece for the collective thematic, stylistic, political, and feminist/womanist concerns that resonate throughout the first phase of Childress's writing career.

Set in the segregated waiting room of a southern railway station, *Florence* begins with the entrance of Mama and her 21-year-old daughter Marge, who seat themselves on the side of the station designated as the "Colored" section. Marge has convinced Mama to journey to New York unannounced to retrieve her other daughter, Florence, whose frustration with southern white oppression, especially since her husband was killed attempting to vote, has motivated her to go north to pursue her dream of becoming a dramatic actress and singer. Florence's attempts have met with little success; the only acting jobs she has landed are those of a maid in a white Broadway production and a part in a film made for a black audience. Unwilling to concede to defeat to northern discrimination, Florence resists returning home.

Critical of her sister's aspirations, Marge believes that Florence does not know her place as a black woman in white America. To her,

Florence's struggle is futile, a pipe dream, since racist whites will never allow blacks equal access to traditionally white-dominated institutions. Her place, from Marge's perspective, is at home rearing her young son, Ted, instead of leaving Mama and herself strapped with the responsibility. Even now she must leave Mama, whose train has not come, to return home to make sure her nephew has not gotten into mischief. Asserting that Florence has "notions a Negro woman don't need," and "must think she's white," Marge instructs Mama to tell Florence that "she ain't gonna feel right no place" (*Florence,* 35, 36).

After Marge exits, Mrs. Carter, "well dressed, wearing furs and carrying a small, expensive overnight bag," breezes in and settles herself in the "White" section (*Florence,* 38). From opposing sides divided by a low railing, the two women engage in conversation about Mrs. Carter's depressed brother, a writer whose book, *Lost My Lonely Way,* has received negative reviews. When Mama finally realizes that the plot of the book centers around a stereotypical, tragic mulatto figure who would rather be dead than have one drop of black blood, she refutes the overworked myth with living testimonies of light-complected blacks whom she personally knows who are proud to affirm their African heritage.

At this juncture, the conversation comes awkwardly to a temporary impasse until Mrs. Carter apologetically rekindles their exchange by asserting that she has liberal sensibilities. Discovering Mama's reason for traveling to New York, Mrs. Carter shares that she, too, is an actress, and although she has "the best of contacts," she has had only a few acting engagements recently. "Of course, I'm not counting the things I just wouldn't do," she adds (*Florence,* 43). Belief in Mrs. Carter's self-proclaimed liberalism and promising theater connections prompts Mama to petition the white woman's aid in securing theater work for Florence. Expressing her moral obligation to help, Mrs. Carter gives Mama the telephone number of Melba Rugby, the director of an upcoming New York musical who is in need of a maid. She offers to contact Rugby personally to recommend Florence, stating, "I'll just tell her no heavy washing or ironing . . . just light cleaning and a little cooking . . . does she cook?" (*Florence,* 45).

Mrs. Carter's unexpected racial condescension provokes Mama's rage; she clutches Mrs. Carter's wrist tightly, causing her discomfort. Intimidated by Mama's unexpected aggressiveness, Mrs. Carter, once she is freed, retreats to the "White Ladies" room. Mama's rage signifies an epiphany. Instead of going to New York, she sends Florence the check that was to have paid for her daughter's return fare home along with the encouraging message: "Keep trying" (*Florence,* 47).

Symbolism Critical commentaries of *Florence* have largely focused on the play's racial symbols. As Elizabeth Brown-Guillory notes, the one-act play "is fraught with potent symbols and symbolic gestures that serve as signposts to the play's main idea."[5] That main idea, which critic Samuel A. Hay posits and Brown-Guillory affirms, is the recognition that "Black people—not white liberals—must struggle if there is to be real political and economic equality."[6]

The mise-en-scène of *Florence* plays a powerful role in establishing the play's social context and texture by replicating on stage what was a clear and present reality across America. Blacks could not legally enter by the same doors as whites, drink from the same water fountains, or refresh themselves in the public "white" rest rooms that they were often responsible for cleaning. The "Colored" and "White" signs placed over the doorways on stage "point to the separate and unequal treatment of blacks," while the railing segregating the station serves "as a physical and emotional barrier" between the two races. On one level, the railing symbolizes the need for blacks to "cross the line" through protest to secure their human rights. On another level, the railing suggests that restrictions that isolate African Americans also limit whites' knowledge of them, thereby perpetuating racial ignorance and stereotypes (Brown-Guillory, 55).

The signs/symbols appearing on the doors of the four rest rooms positioned on stage also support Childress's theme of racial inequality. The inscriptions of "Ladies" and "Gentlemen" on the doors of the white rest rooms suggest "grace, culture, wealth, or royalty" (Brown-Guillory, 54). In stark contrast, the doors of the rest rooms for blacks, void of any suggestion of gentility, simply read "Colored men" and "Colored women." During the course of her wait in the train station, the porter informs Mama that the colored women's rest room is out of order; therefore, she must use the colored men's room. Under Jim Crow law, race overrides gender, making it illegal for her to use the rest room reserved for white women. Brown-Guillory postulates that "the out-of-order rest room becomes a symbol of the black woman's historical burden in America . . . . This play on words hints that for Colored women, there is no room for rest" (55).

The train station setting is also central to the play's racial theme. As is frequently the case in African American literature, "the railway becomes a symbol of escape, conjuring up the Underground Railroad that helped runaway slaves get to the North" (Brown-Guillory, 55). In all likelihood, Florence probably fled the South via this very train.

"The Thwarted Female Artist" and "the Motif of the Journey"   In contrast to many of the plays by African American women dramatists of the first half of the twentieth-century, *Florence* reflects a fusion of literary genres in its intertextuality and an evolving black female consciousness in its feminist ideology. Throughout her canon, Childress's plays read like novels and her novels, in turn, read like plays. The reported, first-person dramatic episodes of Mildred Johnson in *Like One of the Family* and the present-tense narrations of Cora James in *A Short Walk* are as theatrically steeped as the dialogue in *Wedding Band* and *Trouble in Mind.*

Childress's intertwining of themes and styles familiar to both genres suggests a strong influence of past and contemporary twentieth-century black female writers and the sharing of a strong psychic, spiritual, and experiential bond with her racial literary sisters. The fiction of female novelists from the Harlem Renaissance, such as Jessie Fauset, Nella Larsen, and Zora Neale Hurston, to Ann Petry of the mid-1940s, to Alice Walker, Toni Morrison, and Gloria Naylor of the present contains a number of intertextual parallels that are also evident in Childress's work.

As Deborah E. McDowell states in "New Directions for Black Feminist Criticism," "the theme of the thwarted female artist" and "the motif of the journey" figure prominently in the writings of black women.

As thwarted artists, black female characters suffer from repressed and idle imaginations and denial of the opportunity to demonstrate their artistry. And unlike the implicitly political and social journey taken by the black male characters of black male writers, which often involves a "descent into the underworld," the black female's journey, "though at times touching the political and social, is basically personal and psychological." In the works of black women, the female character "is in a state of becoming 'part of an evolutionary spiral, moving from victimization to consciousness.'"[7]

Despite Florence's physical absence in the play proper, her functional "presence" as the eponymous offstage controlling character elevates her, in a figurative sense, to the position of central character in the play. As thwarted artist, she has been racially barred from freely practicing her art form. From the conversation between Mama and Marge, one learns that Florence is financially foundering. For two weeks, she has played the part of a domestic "sweepin" in a white Broadway production and, as the train station porter reports, acted in a black-produced film. She has had marginal success entering the theater as a stage actress largely because of the scarcity of black roles, the demeaning nature of many of those roles, and the racist casting practices that exclude people of color. Leading roles are written for whites and ensemble casts are primarily interpreted as white.

Sue-Ellen Case, in *Feminism and the Theatre,* elaborates on the dyad of marginalization and what she calls ghettoization that Florence's two acting jobs represent. "Florence is relegated to the same role in theatre production as her black counterpart plays in the society at large—the role of the maid. Additionally, her role in the theatre reflects the same class bias as that suffered by the maid: the role is a marginal one, ensuring relative invisibility and bringing paltry financial reward. Florence's other option for work is to be ghettoised, separated from the dominant culture—she can find work in all-black productions."[8]

Florence's psychological journey starts well before her physical journey from South to North. She was no longer willing to defer to the oppressive status quo of white patriarchy in her southern township. But the consequence of defying Jim Crow law would be deadly, as the murder of her husband at the hands of a white mob attests. Challenging institutionalized racism, Florence, before going north, applied for a position as a salesgirl at Strumley's, a store employing whites only. The store, of course, denies her work, but this challenge to racial segregation is perhaps her first premeditated step toward protesting black discrimination and victimization.

Florence's journey mirrors both the archetypal northern migration of runaway slaves and the mass exodus of blacks freed by the Emancipation Proclamation from the agrarian South to the industrialized centers of the North, such as New York, Philadelphia, and Chicago. Her movement from the South to the North represents a quest for physical liberation as well as a conscious emergence of her own psychological autonomy.

Mama, as the main onstage protagonist of the play, takes several figurative and literal journeys. As Brown-Guillory writes, "The cross-country trip that . . . [she and Mrs. Carter] are going on parallels the cross-cultural trip that they take each time the railing is crossed. These women step in and out of each other's cultures as they try to communicate their limitations" (Brown-Guillory, 56).

As Mama anticipates embarking on the same physical journey taken by Florence, her encounter with Mrs. Carter activates her own psychological journey toward a heightened sense of self and other. The mission of her journey north is to bring to an end Florence's journey toward self-assertion and fulfillment, but she is not committed to this mission.

Mama's past approach to life has been to endure whatever hand is dealt her. Falling on a psychological continuum between Marge and Florence, Mama is initially capable of neither passive acceptance nor active resistance to white racism. When Mrs. Carter condescendingly offers to help Florence obtain work as a domestic, Mama's consciousness, perhaps for the first time, expands, bringing long-suppressed anger to the surface. She must act as the empowerer of her daughter instead of relying on someone who is in a position of strength but is unwilling to look beyond differences of class and race to help.

The Myth of Sisterhood and Anger as Illumination Of the four works central to Childress's first writing phase, *Florence* launches her indictment of white women as principal practitioners of racism and classism against members of their own gender, black women. Childress's structuring of the race-gender hierarchy adheres to the traditional pecking order discussed by Zora Neale Hurston, Toni Morrison, and other black women writers, which positions white women above black males and females and places black women subordinately on the bottom rung of power. Childress explodes the myth of sisterhood and the rhetoric of political solidarity that imply that the victimization and oppression common to women of all colors binds them together. Using the anger of black women to challenge white women's exploitation and oppression of women unlike themselves, Childress transforms difference—through insight—into power.

The bourgeois Mrs. Carter exhibits racism and classism throughout her conversation with Mama. First, as southern racist, classist manners and linguistic deference dictate, she introduces herself formally as "Mrs. Carter," yet never asks Mama's surname or Christian name. She requests that Mama dispense with the formality of calling her "Mam" but does not invite true informality by offering her less formal first name.

Second, in the discussion of the tragic mulatto she invokes white patriarchal authority over female and racial authority by implying that a white male, in this case her brother, knows more about the emotions and experiences of black people in general and black women specifically than a black woman does. Mama's failure to receive Mrs. Carter's racist opinion deferentially disturbs the white woman.

Third, Mrs. Carter, stereotyping blacks, responds "pleasantly" to hearing of Florence's aspirations as a singer; "Your people have such a gift. I love spirituals," she comments (*Florence,* 43). Nevertheless, she resists the thought that Florence might be excellent for a part in Melba Rugby's upcoming New York musical. She herself has had nominal success in a male-controlled theater but is still unwilling to help another woman. If Rugby is of a similar racist mindset, she is nothing more than a full-blown composite of Mrs. Carter. Described as "a most versatile woman" who "[w]rites, directs, acts . . . [and does] everything" (*Florence,* 45), Rugby is capable of empowering theater women of all colors, but Mrs. Carter's response implies that she apparently chooses to imitate the racist and sexist behavior of her male peers.

Last, Mrs. Carter projects class bias in her interpretation of "security" for Florence (*Florence,* 46). Working long hours cleaning, cooking, washing, and being the primary caregiver for the children of another household in exchange for a single room, meals that must be eaten alone in the kitchen, low wages, separation from her own family, and limited leisure time surely is not the way that Mrs. Carter defines "security" for herself.

In venting her anger Mama becomes able to revise her racial orientation, which until the moment she clutches Mrs. Carter's wrist has been ideologically flawed. Previously she has deferred to women in Mrs. Carter's class, partly because both de jure and de facto segregation have mandated that she do so and partly because she has been brainwashed into believing that women of Mrs. Carter's social status, since they had more, knew more, and were reputed to be more, were indeed *more*—and more meant better. Mama has also erroneously superimposed her own truly liberal sensibilities onto all women. Now, for perhaps the first time, she sees clearly the moral blindness, the social ambiguities, and the intellectual immaturity of the Mrs. Carters of the world. To underscore the moment of her psychic illumination, Childress has Mama sit quietly and stare straight ahead for several seconds.

Breaking respectful silence, Mama then angrily pulls Mrs. Carter off balance, reproaching her with the diminutive "Child!" (*Florence,* 46), quite the antithesis of her earlier respectful "Mam." Her anger unlocks her understanding and locates her voice—"You better get over on the other side of that rail," she commands Mrs. Carter (*Florence,* 46)—and serves as a catalyst for personal change. No longer indecisive about the role she must play in Florence's dream, she chooses to empower, not disempower, her daughter, realizing that she cannot rely on the kinship of gender to assist Florence. As woman aiding and empowering woman, Mama is the figurative "sister" of the play. The literal sister, Marge, reinforcing white patriarchism and disdainful of her biological sister's strivings, constructs an ideologically segregated sisterhood as well.

Trouble in Mind

In the satiric metadrama *Trouble in Mind,*[9] a play about the theater and a play within a play, Childress expands her exploration of racism and sexism in mid-twentieth-century America. First produced in 1955 and then reworked in 1957, *Trouble in Mind* is weighted with allusions to places and incidents associated with the turbulent civil rights movement that began in the 1950s: to Montgomery, Alabama, the cradle of the Confederacy, where on 1 December 1955 Rosa Parks's refusal to give up her bus seat to accommodate a white person touched off an 11-month bus boycott; to Martin Luther King, the young charismatic Baptist minister who lead the boycott; and to the enrollment in 1957 of nine black students at the all-white Central High School in Little Rock, Arkansas, enforced by the National Guard. These references set the tone for the thematic conflict of the play: passive acceptance versus protest and active resistance.

The inner play addresses much the same kind of racial conflict that early black women dramatists writing between the World Wars used as their artistic and political platform. Many of the racial inequities that Angelina Weld Grimké, Georgia Douglas Johnson, Myrtle Smith Livingston, Alice Dunbar-Nelson, Mary Burrill, and others protested still menaced black Americans a quarter of a century later. In 1955, the same year that *Trouble in Mind* appeared at the Greenwich Mews Theatre, Mississippi authorities pulled from the Tallahatchie River the mutilated and shot-through-the-head body of Emmett Louis Till, a 14-year-old black Chicago native. Two white Mississippi men, later acquitted by an all-white jury of the gruesome kidnap-slaying, had abducted and lynched Till for reportedly flirting with a white woman in a store. It should also be remembered that throughout the South, prior to the Voting Rights Act of 1965, whites denied masses of black men and women the right to vote but did not hesitate to conscript black men for military service. Despite the seeming datedness of the racial conflict over voting of the inner play, Childress was reminding white and black audiences across America that there was still much unconstitutional and inhuman race business in need of disclosure and eradication.

The frame play of *Trouble in Mind* begins with the gathering of a racially mixed cast in a Broadway theater in the mid-1950s to rehearse an antilynching drama, *Chaos in Belleville,* written by a white playwright, Ted Bronson. The black members of the cast are Wiletta Mayer, a middle-aged, self-taught, veteran actress; John Nevins, a neophyte to the professional stage who has studied acting; Millie Davis, an experienced, 35-year-old actress disillusioned by her typecasting in "Aunt Jemima" roles; and Sheldon Forrester, an aged character actor who is committed to placating whites. Completing the ensemble are the white members: Henry, an elderly Irish doorman; Judy Sears, a Yale drama school gradu- ate and idealistic northern liberal; Al Manners, a racist, patronizing Hollywood type in his early 40s who is directing his first Broadway pro- duction; Eddie Fenton, the stage manager; and Bill O'Wray, the only actor of the cast who, because of his race and gender, receives steady employment.

Wiletta, Sheldon, and to some extent Millie, older and experienced, have been conditioned to concede Uncle Tomishly to the white power structure of the theater to ensure themselves continued employment. To them has been bequeathed the spy-in-the-enemy's-country legacy artic- ulated in the deathbed confession of the grandfather in Ralph Ellison's *Invisible Man*. While the white cast members each have only one role to play—that designated in the inner play—the veteran black actors and actresses have a second; it is, as Ellison writes, "to overcome 'em [the whites in charge] with yeses, undermine 'em with grins, agree 'em to death and destruction."[10] Wiletta passes on the subversive legacy of sur- vival—to "laugh at everything they say" to make them feel superior—to John, who, arriving shortly after she enters, dislikes her counsel of self- effacement to whites (*Trouble*, 139). After all are present except Bill, the conflict of the play develops when Manners requires Wiletta personally to justify the actions of Ruby, the role assigned her as an uneducated mother and sharecropper in *Chaos in Belleville*.

Written as a modern plantation drama, *Chaos in Belleville* centers around Mr. Renard (Bill), the white master figure; his southern belle daughter, Miss Carrie (Judy); and their black servants Petunia (Millie), Sam (Sheldon) and his wife, Ruby (Wiletta), and their son, Job (John). Asserting his manhood and citizenship, Job, who has just received notifi- cation that he has been drafted into the armed services, is determined to exercise his Fifteenth Amendment right to vote. Sam and Ruby, fearful of white reprisal against their son's manly defiance, attempt to dissuade him, but Job is resolute. In response, a white mob forms to lynch him for his "wrongdoing" in daring to vote. Ruby advises her son that "[t]here's only one right thing to do! . . . You got to go and give yourself up" (*Trouble*, 161–62). Job's repeated declaration that he has done nothing illegal goes unheard. Duty bound to protect her colored people, Miss

Carrie gains her father's support to escort Job to the county jail, where he will be safe, but en route deputies detain them and one of them shoots and kills Job as he flees from their restraint. Protesting lynching, Renard proceeds to make those responsible for Job's death feel guilt-stricken for taking the life of an innocent man.

Unable to justify Ruby's choice to send her son out into the teeth of a lynch mob, Wiletta calls the play a lie, stating that a mother, no matter how poor or uneducated, would never send her son out to his death. Furthermore, she comprehends that Bronson intends to make a white man, Renard, the hero of the play, while casting the black mother as inept and villainous. Angered at being asked once again to compromise her intelligence and artistic sensibilities for the purpose of presenting herself (and so black women) in a blatantly invalid light, Wiletta sacrifices her job to give voice to her convictions and to truth. Calling for a revision of the play's ending, Wiletta asks Manners if he would send his son to be murdered. His racist reply loses him the company's support and respect: "Don't compare yourself to me! What goes for my son doesn't necessarily go for yours! Don't compare him (*Points to JOHN.*) . . . with three strikes against him, don't compare him with my son, they've got nothing in common . . . not a Goddam thing!" (*Trouble,* 171).

The play concludes with the abrupt dismissal of the cast for the day and the instruction that they will be telephoned about tomorrow's rehearsal. Failing to gain the support of the other black cast members because they need the work, Wiletta surmises that in telephoning each member of the ensemble Manners's plan is "to divide and conquer"; she knows that she will not be called. Already risking professional suicide, she decides "to show up any damn way" to resist Bronson's unrealistic script until Manners concedes or fires her (*Trouble,* 173).

Bronson's *Chaos in Belleville* is reminiscent of the "black" melodramas of the 1920s and 1930s written by whites that repeatedly endorse an image of blacks as childlike and helpless. Without the watchful guardianship of white master and mistress, the black characters are dysfunctional, even in matters where maternal and paternal instincts govern. Childress clearly maintains that servile, God-fearing, illiterate blacks who respond with a sigh, a hum, and a prayer of "Lord, have mercy!" are the only blacks that white America wishes to acknowledge. The "Broadway Shuffle" that she satirically protests adumbrates filmmaker Robert Townsend's comic protest 30 years later of the "Hollywood Shuffle" that cast the black performing artist as either devoted, mindless servant or sexual dynamo, as Mammy or Mandingo.[11]

As with the discussion of *Lost My Lonely Way* in *Florence,* Childress again uses a white-authored fictional work within her drama to affirm a message of black home rule. First, Childress reiterates that white males are not in a position to know black women and men better than they know themselves. Second, as long as "the man" (that is, the white man as figured by the character "Man-ners") controls every aspect of the theater as producer, director, playwright, theater owner, and critic, blacks will be at the mercy of his interpretation, his parameters for their inclusion and exclusion. And last, the definition and preservation of realistic and truthful black drama will largely depend on racially informed dramatists, actors, and audiences, both black and white, committed to endorsing true portraits of black people and their experiences.

Thwarted Theater Artists In a sense, all the black actors in *Trouble in Mind* are thwarted artists. They are asked to perform in *Chaos in Belleville* stock actions all too familiar in plays about black life written by whites. While waiting to hear the outcome of Job's voting, Sheldon's character, Sam, whittles on a stick, Wiletta's Ruby irons, and Millie as Petunia constantly looks out the window. Being limited to uttering fragmented sentences, to praying, and to singing spirituals deprives black actors and actresses of the opportunity to showcase their range of talents. Illustrative of the repetitive typecasting that black actresses experience is the habitual naming of their characters after gems, such as Sapphire, Pearl, Opal, Crystal, and Ruby, or after flowers, such as Gardenia, Magnolia, Chrysanthemum, and Petunia. Moreover, their standard costuming as "handkerchief heads"—wearing bandanna headwraps and frumpy cotton dresses—restricts them to portraying narrowly defined underclass and anti-intellectual types.

All of the above notwithstanding, Wiletta, undergoing a personal psychological journey from conformist to individualist, is the frustrated artist evolving from passive acceptance to conscious resistance. Early in act 1, Wiletta comments to John that "*show business* . . . [is] just a business" and that "Colored folks ain't in no theatre" (*Trouble,* 139). Her wry pronouncement indicates that the roles blacks are expected to perform, in addition to being false, lack aesthetic grounding; they are sterile renderings executed for commercial exchanges between employer and performing artist and theater and paying public. Never in the truest sense has she been given the opportunity to perform as a serious professional. After more than 20 years in the business, her goal in life is still to *become* an actress.

Wiletta's Anger and Protest In the original three-act version of *Trouble in Mind* performed in 1955, Wiletta rallies the cast to her cause, leads a walk-out in protest of the racially biased script, and Manners has a change of heart. According to Case, ending with cast solidarity "suggests that a black political consciousness and protest can be applied to the institution of the theatre" and "also depicts the positive role the expression of anger can play among peers, as the actor successfully gains support from the other members of her cast" (101). The 1957 two-act published version, ending in Wiletta's solitary challenge to the theater's white patriarchy, no less illuminates the powerful potential of anger to effect change.

Wiletta's expression of repressed anger becomes a key component of the plot in the first act. Being "nice" in order to preserve her job, she has accumulated a storehouse of unconscious rage. Her expression of anger is inevitable, as her professional life has consisted of giving in and going along. Having a job has been more important than having a self. When Manners insists that Wiletta pick up a paper he has thrown across the stage, her vituperative response, "Well, hell! I ain't the damn janitor!" stuns him and the others (*Trouble,* 146). Surprised and embarrassed by her caustic reply, Manners deceptively passes off Wiletta's response as Method acting by announcing that what they "have just seen is . . . is . . . is fine acting. . . . You gave me anger, frustration, movement, er . . . excitement" (*Trouble,* 146).

Manners is ill-equipped to deal with Wiletta's anger because he lacks experience responding to the aggressive emotions of a black woman and perhaps any woman. The thinly sketched details of his failed marriage and his determination to avoid communication with his exwife strongly suggest the latter. Wiletta, reared in a culture that disallows women the public display of anger, has until her outburst blinded Manners to her true emotional self. Her public demonstration of anger is a foreign phenomenon, an aspect of her self with which he has not had to deal, and with which he cannot deal since it is a challenge to his white paternalism. Manners counters Wiletta's self-assertion with avoidance, silencing, and dismissal. When attempts to busy himself with other actors fail to stifle her voice and her challenges to his authority, he resorts to condescending attacks on her intellect. To her questioning of the racist, sexist plot of *Chaos in Belleville,* he responds, "Darling, don't think. You're great until you start thinking. I don't expect you to. . . . Make me a solemn promise, don't start thinking" (*Trouble,* 157).

The blues song for which the play is titled, "Trouble in Mind," connotes the psychic dilemma Wiletta confronts in thinking through her choice of protest over passivity. Indeed, during the course of the play, thinking becomes a revolutionary act. An upset Wiletta at the end of act 1 confides to Henry, the Irish doorman, that she dislikes thinking because it makes her "fightin' mad. . . . I take and take, then watch out!" (*Trouble*, 153–54). Wiletta's "business" approach to acting in the white man's theater has legitimized the compromise of her talent, stifled her thinking, and resulted in a silencing and abnegation of self.

Manners's request for the justification of an unrealistic, unnatural maternal act forces Wiletta to think through the racist script not in an abstract, depersonalized way but in a concrete, personal manner. Her frustration with him enables her to make connections between herself and her character, Ruby, who is not expected to think for herself either. When Manners challenges Judy and Millie's objection to the word "darkies" in *Chaos in Belleville* by polling the other member of the cast, Wiletta disturbingly retreats into ignorance. She hears herself echoing Ruby's scripted line, "Lord, have mercy, don't ask me 'cause I don't know" (*Trouble*, 147). The thinking through of her accountability in acting out the bogus plot on stage as well in her daily life marks the beginning of her protest.

Wiletta's venting of anger has transformative, liberating power. Her vehement denunciation of Bronson's script transforms her from passivity to protest, from white accommodation to black affirmation, from self-imposed and other-imposed silence to speech. Moreover, her anger reconfigures the authorial and authoritative structure in *Trouble in Mind* from male to female, from white to black, and from black woman as object to black woman as subject. Angered at her own complicity in aiding and abetting whites' objectification and stereotyping of her race, Wiletta reclaims control of characterizing the black female in order to re-create her in her own true image. Her evolution from renderer of false, other-imposed image to shaper of true, self-constructed image recasts her role in the work as actress-turned-dramatist. Wiletta's revolt is one ripple in a sea of exclusion and discrimination, but it is a crucial ripple toward building a tidal wave of resistance. She actualizes her ambition "to do somethin' real grand . . . in the theater . . . to stand forth at my best . . . to stand up here and do anything I want" (*Trouble*, 173).

Like One of the Family

By and large, black domestics have been depicted as aged, obese, asexual, pious women who, in addition to being adoring of whites, long-suffering, passive, and submissive, are physically and emotionally resilient. Their perceived strength, which is often shown in contrast to weak, ineffectual white women, abounds in the fiction of both blacks and whites. Childress's presentation of the black domestic breaks with the popularized self-effacing mammy portrait. Totally self-willed, Childress's characterization reveals the multifaceted personality, wit, and intellectual savvy of this everyday figure who was often reputed to be of limited mental scope. She depicts the black maid's life apart from domestic service and the human as well as the inhuman side of domestic employment. Also shown is the humor as well as the rage attached to being expected to exchange dignity for pay.

Mildred Johnson, the 32-year-old black maid from South Carolina who narrates the 62 dramatic monologues in *Like One of the Family . . . Conversations from a Domestic's Life* (1956), is neither the loud, bossy, faithful mammy figure duty bound to take care of a weak, ineffectual mistress nor the childlike, simpleminded Prissy type from *Gone With the Wind* who has to be reprimanded at every turn. Mildred herself complains of being much too acquainted with film depictions of the former type:

> As soon as I see a colored maid that's workin' for somebody, I know that she will have a coniption-fit 'cause the lady she works for won't eat her dinner and before long the maid will say, "You eatin' just like a bird!" Or, "Somethin's worryin' you, chile, and I won't rest 'til I find out what it is!" I know that maids don't be carryin' on like that over the people they work for, at least none of 'em that I've ever met![12]

Recounting her experiences of living in New York City and working as a domestic in the homes of white women during the 1950s, Mildred depicts herself professionally as an iconoclast. Bowing and scraping, feigning the humble slave act, is not part of her job description. She freely speaks her mind when an employer abuses the work relationship or insults her intelligence and dignity as a human being. Because she does not rely on a single household for employment, does not commit herself to live-in service, does not accept service pans (leftover food) or cast-off clothing, and does not have dependents whose support would constrict her autonomy in speech and movement, Mildred's direct, sassy redress to confrontation is more believable.

Moreover, Mildred's personal profile transcends the overworked portrait of the zealous fundamentalist drudge, who goes through life either manhandled or manless, running a gauntlet of tribulations that she will

understand better by and by. Not overly religious, Mildred admits in "I
Go to Church" that she rarely attends services. When she does elect to
go, however, she chides the minister for his obsessive preaching of
somber sermons. Her life is not null and void. She has her own apartment and a steady, supportive man in her life who does not fit into the
"he ain't much good, but I guess he's all I got" mold (*Like One,* 123). She
knows black history and is politically aware of international as well as
national race issues. And though she lacks a large discretionary income,
she is able to purchase groceries as gifts for friends.

An engaging mixture of humor, wit, wisdom, indignation, and anger,
the conversations cover an extensive range "that others," as Trudier
Harris points out, "might judge antithetical to a domestic's intellectual
ken" (Harris 1986, xvii). A revisionist look at black history is the topic of
"I Visit Yesterday," "The 'Many Others' in History," "History in the
Makin," and "All about Miss Tubman." The uplift of the profession, the
need for domestic solidarity and work reform, and the common sisterhood of all maids are the subjects of "All about My Job," "We Need a
Union Too," and "In the Laundry Room." The effects of racism versus
the effects of racial cooperation and peace make up the thematic nucle-
uses of "Ridin' the Bus," "Got to Go Someplace," "Nasty Compliments,"
"What Is It All About?" "Merry Christmas, Marge!" "A New Kind of
Prayer," "If Heaven Is What We Want," "Missionaries," "The
Benevolent Club," and "The A B C's of Life and Learning." In "Bubba"
and "Discontent," Mildred advocates public protest as a method of
effecting racial and social change.

"Dance with Me, Henry" and "Men in Your Life" indict the sexist
behavior of men toward women based on their physicality. Confronting
ageism, demythifying the belief that the North is the promised land for
blacks, and refuting the idea that individual blacks must obligatorily
carry the burdens of the entire race are the themes of "Old as the Hills,"
"Northerners Can Be So Smug," and "Why Should I Get Upset?" "I Go
to a Funeral" and "Good Reason for a Good Time" focus on the benefits
of communal sharing. Satirical indictments of the theater and
Hollywood's misrepresentation of men of color and women are the subjects of "About Those Colored Movies" and "I Could Run a School Too."
Three conversations—"What Does Africa Want? . . . Freedom!" and
"Somehow I'd Like to Thank Them" (both monologues of protests
against South Africa's apartheid) as well as "Dope and Things Like That"
(a discussion of the growing drug problem among America's inner city

youths)—affirm the existence of two pernicious social problems long before they became popular causes. "Somehow I'd Like to Thank Them" applauds an act of solidarity in resisting racism by a group of South African white women.

Neutralization of Race In 17 monologues in *Like One of the Family,*[13] Mildred recounts various pleasant and unpleasant episodes that occur in the homes of the white families that hire her for day work. Seven of these monologues focus on her relationships with the white mistresses of these households. The title conversation, "Like One of the Family," serves as a precursor and prototype for "If You Want to Get Along with Me," "The Pocketbook Game," "The Health Card," "Mrs. James," and "On Leaving Notes." Positioned as the first monologue, "Like One of the Family" encodes the verbal and spatial politics that Childress manipulates throughout to equalize the relationships between Mildred and her white female employers.

Conversely, the monologue entitled "I Liked Workin' at that Place" describes the ideal professional and personal relationship between white mistress and black maid, one of mutual respect and flexibility. Childress, using Mildred as her mouthpiece, converts a traditionally unequal relationship into an egalitarian one to demonstrate that racism is not a matter of skin color but of prejudgments and ignorance.

Notably, Mildred does not emphasize her race or the race of the women for whom she works. Her employers' comments and curiosities about black life expose their whiteness. Here, the omission of direct, racial designators expresses a desire not to concentrate on color as the true creator of racial dissonance. The contents of their character, not the color of their skin, dictate Mildred's interactions with the white women for whom she cooks and cleans. Accordingly, Mildred believes that her moral character and professionalism should earn her the respect that she rightfully deserves.

In the sharing of her day-work experiences with Marge—her friend, neighbor, and sister domestic who functions as the sole audience for all 62 conversations—Mildred signifies on the shameless actions of her mistresses but never speaks condescendingly of their whiteness. Although she has the freedom to speak candidly to her racial sister about these women, she comments only on the abrasive or affable qualities of their personalities. In "Like One of the Family," Mildred tells Marge that her mistress, Mrs. C . . . , is a "pretty nice woman" who unfortunately "gripes" her with her ways (*Like One,* 1). Her "ways" include a display of contrived white liberalism before company at Mildred's expense. Regarding her as a voiceless, invisible woman, Mrs. C . . . takes advantage of Mildred's respectful silence. Mildred narrates:

> When she has company, for example, she'll holler out to me from the living room to the kitchen: "Mildred dear! Be sure and eat *both* of those lamb chops for your lunch!" Now you know she wasn't doing a thing but tryin' to prove to the company how "good" and "kind" she was to the servant, because she had told me *already* to eat those chops.
>
> Today she had a girl friend of hers over to lunch and I was real busy afterwards clearing the things away and she called me over and introduced me to the woman. . . . Oh no, Marge! I didn't object to that at all. I greeted the lady and then went back to my work. . . . And then it started! I could hear her talkin' just as loud . . . and she says to her friend, "We *just* love her! She's *like* one of the family and she *just adores* our little Carol! We don't know *what* we'd do without her! We don't think of her as a servant!" And on and on she went . . . and every time I came in to move a plate off the table both of them would grin at me like chessy cats. (1–2)

Allowing racialized situations to speak for themselves without emphasizing race, Childress has Mildred throughout contend with correcting white women's racial stereotypes of blacks and the familiar behavior that they exhibit toward her. For example, believing all blacks to be dishonest, Mrs. E . . . in "The Pocketbook Game" will not put down her purse for fear that Mildred will steal her money. Mildred checks the insult by pretending to dash back to Mrs. E . . .'s apartment to secure her own purse after her employer has hurriedly sent her on an errand to intercept the superintendent of the building before he leaves.

Her mistress in "The Health Card," regarding blacks as diseased, requests medical certification to prove that Mildred is physically fit to work in her home. Mildred reverses the insulting stereotype by requesting health cards for every member of her employer's family, since handling their laundry and linen presumably puts her equally at risk.

In "On Leavin' Notes," Mrs. R . . . views Mildred as cheap labor that can be used to her economic advantage. Leaving a note containing a request that she would not make to Mildred's face, Mrs. R . . . expects Mildred—outside of their service agreement—to wash three of her cotton housecoats for $1 while the corner laundry charges 75 cents per coat. Mildred puts Mrs. R . . . on notice to never leave her exploitative notes again. Mrs. M . . . in "If You Want to Get Along with Me" thinks she can pry into Mildred's intimate and monetary affairs and go to her place of residence uninvited. Mildred has to remind Mrs. M . . . that she does not share a reciprocal familiarity with her.

Neutralization of Names The conversation entitled "Mrs. James" illustrates the power and control that names, marital titles, and patronymics play in creating space and distance between white employer and black employee. Mildred narrates to Marge the following encounter with Mrs. James, who unfailingly refers to herself in third-person:

> WELL MARGE, you haven't heard anything! You should hear the woman I work for . . . she's really something. Calls herself "Mrs. James!" All the time she says "Mrs. James."
>
> The first day I was there she come into the kitchen and says, "Mildred, Mrs. James would like you to clean the pantry." Well I looked 'round to see if she meant her mother-in-law or somebody and then she adds, "If anyone calls, Mrs. James is out shopping." And with that she sashays out the door.
>
> Now she keeps on talking that way all the time, the whole time I'm there. That woman wouldn't say "I" or "me" for nothing in the world. The way I look at it . . . I guess she thought it would be too personal.
>
> Now Marge, you know I don't work Saturdays for nobody! Well sir! Last Friday she breezed in the kitchen and fussed around a little . . . movin' first the salt and then the pepper, I could feel something brewin' in the air. Next thing you know she speaks up. "Mildred," she says, "Mrs. James will need you this Saturday." I was polishin' silver at the time but I turned around and looked her dead in the eye and said, "Mildred does not work on Saturdays." (*Like One,* 60)

Mrs. James's choice of formal self-naming and her avoidance of first-person referents disallow the personal and the familiar. She objectifies her name and, in turn, herself as a separate entity, as something she can psychologically set apart. Mrs. James, however, lacks no compunction to address Mildred directly, informally by her first name, and without respectfully accrediting her a title. Transforming name and self linguistically into distant objects, she creates a social chasm between the two of them. Believing herself to be superior, Mrs. James clearly objectifies Mildred as other, as a representative of both a subordinate class and inferior caste. Since their relationship as mistress and maid, besides being an inequitable one, lacks mutual respect, Mrs. James's calling of Mildred by her first name is humiliatingly reductive. Mildred's response in imitation of Mrs. James, in addition to being humorous, exposes the ridiculous nature of racism and classism and neutralizes the artificial distance that Mrs. James strains to impose.

Aside from the conversation "Mrs. James," which centers directly on the racist and classist use of names, "The Health Card" is the only other conversation that contains the full patronymic of a mistress, Mrs. Jones, and it appears only once. Trudier Harris, in *From Mammies to Militants,* asserts that Mildred's "changing [of] names to protect privacy" heightens the verisimilitude of the monologues.[14] Furthermore, the abbreviations of her mistresses' patronymics allows Mildred to indict without malice not a single individual but rather a representative type guilty of these racist infractions.

Neutralization of Space Mildred equates true friendship, acceptance, and equality with verbal and spatial freedom and knowledge of one's place in both the personal and professional sense. *Place,* in this instance, refers to physical location, psychological orientation, and social status. Mildred's female employers repeatedly violate her personal and professional space, while she, in turn, breaches verbal and spatial boundaries to resist exploitation, take a political stand, or raise her mistresses' class and racial consciousnesses. In "Like One of the Family," Mildred physically neutralizes the social inequity between herself and Mrs. C . . . , who for the sake of a liberal appearance gives her luncheon guest the false impression that Mildred is not regarded as a servant but as a beloved, family member whom she and her family could not do without. Confronting her mistress after the guest leaves, Mildred steps out of her assigned domestic sphere of the kitchen and draws up a chair in the living room dissolving inequity.[15] As she speaks her mind to Mrs. C . . . she breaks the code of domestic silence and does become, briefly, "like one of the family." Mildred's message is direct and simple: treat me with respect and humanity.

Mildred's confrontations with her mistresses illuminate the contradiction, as some of Childress's critics have noted, that blacks should know their place as servants when, ironically, whites do not know theirs as human beings. Both Childress's and Mildred's primary mission is to teach and delight without alienating those whose consciousness they wish to raise. De-emphasizing skin color and neutralizing the verbal and spatial grounds on which racism abounds enable them to accomplish both objectives effectively.

Mildred as Mythologizer and Artist As storyteller, leading actress in the oral re-creations of her daily dramas, and mythologizer of self,

Mildred the domestic doubles as Mildred the artist. Just as Huck Finn tells his own adventures, ostensibly effacing Mark Twain's authorial voice, artistic control, and sociopolitical ideology, Mildred affords Childress the semblance of total authorial absence from *Like One of the Family*. As the presiding presence of Childress recedes, Mildred, in turn, accedes to the position of sole author of a theatrical, one-woman show. A nontraditional artist, Mildred uses spoken words as her paints and crayons, and her canvas is her own imagination and the imaginations of her listeners, Marge and the readers of her recorded performances.

Trudier Harris posits that Mildred, as a practitioner of the black folk tradition, a tradition that demands listener participation and response (ellipses indicate when Marge has presumably made a comment) and that allows performance and recitation without interfering with daily tasks, effects immediacy and the appearance of artlessness in her monologues and conversations. There is no distinction between art as life and art as artifact, the two being inextricably fused. In the absence of leisure time to compose written texts, settings such as the kitchen, the porch, and the living room and domestic activities such as shelling beans, kneading bread, and ironing clothes become for women, and especially for Mildred, spheres for oral composition.[16]

The major side effect of Mildred's ostensibly serving as the sole shaper of her own experiences is the potential for unreliable narration. Comparable with the first-person narration of Huck Finn, which allows him the appearance of an uncontrolled, authorial consciousness and reveals him to be an unreliable explicator of character and incident because of his youth and innocence, Mildred's conversations reporting her boldness with her employers and members of the black community strain her credibility. The reader, along with Marge, seriously doubts that Mildred snatches a paper out of Mrs. B . . .'s hand ("Ain't You Mad?"), sits down uninvited in the living room of Mrs. C . . . "and read[s] her thusly" ("Like One of the Family"), or criticizes the sermons of her minister to his face ("I Go to Church"). Surely in Mildred's creation of an autonomous self, particularly an autonomous, bold self, she would be unlikely to recite an episode that would reveal her to be as narrow-minded and as bigoted as those whom she confronts.

The *truth* in the conversations of Mildred is the exemplum of morality each portrays, not the exact reportage of what happened. "[M]etaphoric truth subverts the literalness of the situation presented" (Harris 1980, 27). Moreover, Mildred as unreliable narrator continues the black oral tradition popularized by the tellers of Staggolee tales, who appropriate the legendary figure's sexual and masculine prowess by adopting the "intrusive I" in their self-laudatory "toasts," or poetic tributes.[17] First-person narration substitutes for third-person point of view. Transforming herself from literary object to subject, Mildred mythologizes herself.

"Ain't You Mad?" Mildred as artist rechannels her anger at being treated like a second-class citizen. In the majority of her confrontations with white mistresses, she is emotionally in control. Her satire, in addition to raising the consciousness of her fictive mistresses, is designed to prick the conscience of her white readers while exorcising the anger of the black maids and butlers who have been victimized by similar dehumanizing acts. Helen Davis, in her review of *Like One of the Family,* notes that anger is the key emotional response to the conversations. Childress, via Mildred, "*does* move the reader—to tears and to laughter—but mostly to anger, the kind of anger which is the courage to change and fight against the ugliness surrounding us."[18]

The undercurrent of racialized anger in "Weekend with Pearl," "Let's Face It," and many of the other conversations surfaces most distinctly in "Ain't You Mad?," the only monologue in which Mildred abandons her calm, morally persuasive persona. Sacrificing her usual witty handling of a racially charged situation for an emotional display, Mildred argues with both her mistress and her mistress's husband, becomes physically agitated, is sent home by her employers, and loses the opportunity to sensitize two passive racists. Paradoxically, the vignette "is striking . . . in that it is the least realistic confrontation in the conversations, yet it has the most realistic, least optimistic ending" (Harris 1986, xxiv).

Mildred reports to Marge that she is sick to her soul and stomach. Earlier that morning, while Mr. and Mrs. B., her employers, are leisurely finishing their breakfast, Mr. B., looking up from his newspaper, comments that it's "too bad" about a recent attempt of a black girl to integrate Alabama University. Mrs. B. follows up with "tch, tch, tch, I know *you people* [black people] are angry about this. What is going to be done?" The complacent attitudes of both ignite Mildred's temper, but it appears that Mrs. B., especially, antagonizes her. Mildred hollers at her, "What the hamfat is the matter with you? *Ain't you mad?* Now you either be *mad* or *shame,* but don't sit there with your mouth full 'tut-tut-tin' at me! Now if you mad, you'd of told me what *you done* and if you shame, you oughta be hangin' your head instead of smackin' your lips over them goodies!" (*Like One,* 171).

Startled, Mr. B. comes to his wife's defense, instructing Mildred not to upset her and asserting that they "were tryin' to be sympathetic" (*Like One,* 171). Yelling at them both, Mildred makes a sharp distinction between the public support that an upset Mrs. B. would receive and the indifference that would meet her own display of anger and the anger of Autherine Lucy, the young black woman alluded to in the newspaper article.[19] "Don't you worry about Mrs. B. bein' upset 'cause if she gets too wrought up she can *scream* and the law, the klan and them men that ganged up on that young lady to keep her out of school, that's right, every one of 'em will come runnin' in here and move me off the premises piece by piece!" (*Like One,* 172).

Resisting the ugly truth of Mildred's words, Mrs. B. jumps up, threateningly waves a newspaper in her face, and commands Mildred to go home immediately. Mildred snatches the newspaper out of her hand and departs, affirming the right of everyone to a decent life and the moral responsibility of everyone to protect that right. "All those that keep quiet are with the mob whether they agree with 'em or not!," she emphatically proclaims (*Like One,* 173).

Repressed anger at social injustice and whites' interracial apathy are the themes of "Ain't You Mad?" In contrast with the other conversations set during the domestic's work day, here Mildred takes no responsibility for altering the racial psyches of the whites for whom she works but holds them responsible for the state and alteration of their own. She levels her anger first at Mrs. B., since clearly no part of this white woman identifies with a black woman attempting to enter the college of her choice and courageously taking on the status quo in the process. Mrs. B. is indifferent to gender because race obscures the issue of rights and what is right. In her enraged attack on Mrs. B.'s indifference, Mildred implies that had Autherine Lucy been white and the door of a patriarchal institution barred to her based on gender, then letters and acts of protest from incensed white women in every quadrant of the country would have vociferously resisted her expulsion.

Mr. and Mrs. B.'s nonchalant reaction to the ugliness unfolding in Alabama exemplifies not only whites insensitivity and lack of concerned involvement in racialized issues affecting the black community but their indifference to stating and upholding what is morally and constitutionally right when the issue of race is involved. Had Mr. and Mrs. B. listened to the content of Mildred's message with the same intensity as they defended themselves against it and the manner of her presentation, a substantive understanding might have been reached. Reciprocating with anger impedes the reception of the message and renders Mildred's anger inconsequential in comparison with their own. The calm and collected Mildred who is able to proselytize her white employers steps back in "Ain't You Mad?" to reveal another and perhaps truer dimension of the black-white experience and the presence of racial rage that not infrequently boils to the top of that experience.

Wedding Band

Commonly classified as an integrationist drama, *Wedding Band: A Love/Hate Story in Black and White* (1966) has chiefly been critiqued—as is the case with Childress's other works from this phase of her career—on the basis of its racial politics. Set in South Carolina in 1918, the play treats the "four inconsistencies in American society" that early African American women playwrights protested throughout the century's first half. Inscribed in the play are the themes of miscegenation, the white disenfranchisement of the African American soldier, the racially informed poverty of blacks, and the threat of lynching (Brown-Guillory, 5).

Viewing *Wedding Band* as a period play, patrons who attended its first production at the University of Michigan in 1966 and those who saw Joseph Papp's Public Theatre production six years later perhaps regarded its themes as extinct issues, unfortunate events and circumstances of days gone by. But this clearly was not the playwright's intent. In 1966, the same year that *Wedding Band* was first performed, Childress published an article in which she attacked the continued presence of state laws—in South Carolina for one—forbidding miscegenation and interracial marriage.[20] Childress was particularly concerned with the infringement of such laws on the personal lives and freedoms of black women. As she stated elsewhere, "*Wedding Band* dealt with a black woman and a white man, but it was about black women's rights. . . . The play shows society's determination to hold the black woman down through laws framed against her. There are similar laws framed against white women, and, of course, unwritten laws. I never run out of subject matter for writing about women's rights—particularly black women."[21]

Beyond interracial, heterosexual relations and black women's rights, the play's primary assault, as Catherine Wiley asserts, is against the segregated sisterhood among black women and between black women and white women—not only during World War I in South Carolina but across contemporary America. Wiley writes, "Childress's play can be read today as a history lesson pointed at white women to remind them and us, in 1966 or now, that our vision of sisterly equality has always left some sisters out."[22] Childress's "lesson" also indicts "bourgeois" black women who fail to identify with their racial sisters of the lower socioeconomic echelons. As in earlier works of this phase, Childress uses the confrontation of white and black females to detonate anger, which redirects the black female protagonist's energies and heightens her awareness of her true relation to women inside and outside her race.

Act 1 of *Wedding Band* takes place on a South Carolina Saturday morning in the summer of 1918, the tenth anniversary of the "keepin' company" relationship of Julia Augustine, a 35-year-old black seamstress, and Herman, a 40-year-old white baker (*Wedding Band,* 10). The Saturday is also Julia's first day as the backyard tenant in an urban, underclass black community after living a lonely existence in the country and in a middle-class black neighborhood. Julia's small house is situated between the houses of two other female tenants. Mattie, whose husband October is away at sea, and her 8-year-old daughter Teeta rent the house on one side. Lula Green, a motherly 45-year-old widow, and her adopted son Nelson, on leave from the army, rent the other. Their landlady, Fanny Johnson, a 50-year-old busybody, prides herself on being "quality" and the self-appointed standard bearer for the race.

Initially, Julia self-protectively holds herself back from the members of her new community; but they manage to inject themselves into her space. Illiterate Mattie asks Julia to read a letter she has just received from October. The sharing of the private text of the letter transforms it into a communal text, uniting the women. One line of October's letter, "Two things a man can give the woman he loves . . . his name and his protection," is particularly haunting for Julia, since she has gotten neither from Herman, after 10 years of essentially serving as his common-law wife.

The spell of intimacy that the letter casts predisposes Julia to drop her reserve and take the two women into her confidence concerning her affair with Herman, whom she cannot legally marry in South Carolina because he is white and state law forbids miscegenation. Evoking images of the slavemaster who sexually exploited black women, Lula counsels Julia that she should have nothing to do with a white man, whereas Mattie recommends that she exploit Herman for all she can get. The two women then fall silent and return to their houses, refusing to comprehend that Julia's love for Herman is the same as a black woman's love for a black man.

Herman's entrance during the evening scene of the first act clarifies the reason for Julia's dilemma and establishes the source of conflict between Julia and the white women in the play. Herman's mother, whom he views as "a poor, ignorant woman who is mad because she was born a sharecropper . . . outta her mind 'cause she ain't high class society," has nonetheless helped him out by borrowing against their house to finance his bakery shop (*Wedding Band,* 25). He, in turn, has assumed the support of his mother and sister, Annabelle. Thus it is his commitment to them that keeps the couple in the South, where they cannot marry.

Further complicating the situation, Herman's mother is intolerant of his relationship with a black woman. Years earlier, Herman incautiously reported to Julia that his mother called her "nigger," and the memory of the racial slur still stirs Julia's anger. To sabotage their affair, his mother, with the help of Annabelle, tries to lure Herman's affection away from Julia by habitually inviting Celestine, a white widow, to dinner. In response to the manipulative maternal control to which Herman defers, Julia also directs her unacknowledged resentment of Herman onto his mother.

Assuaging her anger, Herman presents Julia with tenth anniversary gifts: a wedding cake and a wide, gold wedding band strung on a chain to wear around her neck until they can go north to marry. He outlines a plan to obtain a ticket to send Julia north on the Clyde Line Boat; he will follow later. Seemingly rising to execute his plan, Herman then abruptly collapses in Julia's home, sick with the influenza that is ravaging the country.

Circumventing South Carolina's laws against miscegenation becomes the problematic issue of act 2, beginning the morning of the next day. The women of the yard are in a double bind regarding how to handle Herman's threatening presence and life-threatening illness. If they summon a doctor, the doctor will be obligated to report the illegal relationship and the couple will be prosecuted. As a consequence, the wrath of the whites in the surrounding communities will be heaped on everyone in the black community. Conversely, for fear of spreading the flu virus, which has reached epidemic proportions, they do not want to transport the stricken Herman.[23] Julia's house must be quarantined. Despite the threat to Herman's life, they cannot call a doctor or move him home or to a hospital without drawing unwanted attention or legal prosecution. As a solution, Julia sends for his sister and mother.

The two white women's initiations into the backyard differ in kind and degree. Arriving first, Annabelle, a woman in her 30s, is nervous but curious in the foreign environment. Despite the awkwardness of the situation, her conversation is laced with "please" and "thank you," particularly where her brother is concerned. "'Course you could put him out," she admits to Julia, but quickly follows with, "Please let us wait 'til dark" (*Wedding Band,* 39). Meanwhile, "assuming" the airs of "quality" and "calm well-being," the 57-year-old mother of Herman surveys the backyard with cold detachment (*Wedding Band,* 43).

Failing to acknowledge Julia's presence as she enters the black woman's house, she immediately devises a tale to explain to the authorities her son's presence in a black woman's bed. "My son comes to deliver baked goods and the influenza strikes him down. Sickness, it's the war," she states (*Wedding Band,* 45). Altering the truth comes easy to her again when she introduces herself as "Mrs. Thelma" instead of "Frieda"; because of the war, she does not want her German ancestry betrayed. Her son needs immediate medical attention, but she refuses to bring a doctor to his bedside and will wait until nightfall to move him. When Annabelle reminds her that they are not obeying the city's quarantine law, Herman's mother emphasizes respectability over the importance of Herman's life: "Let the city drop dead and you 'long with it. *Rather* be dead than disgraced" (*Wedding Band,* 48).

To participate in her own erasure, silencing, and castigation proves intolerable for Julia, who has promised Herman to hold her tongue and tolerate the women of his family. When Herman's mother states that Julia ought to be locked up in the workhouse jail and invokes the stereotypical black female sexual myth at the same moment that Herman deliriously recites a racist Calhoun speech he learned as a child, Julia loses her composure and her temper. Agitated by his mother's insulting, rhetorical question—"Who you think you are?"—Julia launches into the following diatribe:

> I'm your damn daughter-in-law, you old bitch! . . . The black thing who bought a hot water bottle to put on your sick, white self when rheumatism threw you flat on your back . . . who bought flannel gowns to warm your pale, mean body. He never ran up and down King Street shoppin' for you . . . I bought what he took home to you . . . the lace curtain in your parlor . . . the shirt-waist you wearin'—I made them. . . . If I wasn't black with all-a Carolina 'gainst me I'd be mistress of your house!

Annabelle, you'd be married livin' in Brooklyn, New York . . . and I'd be
waitin' on Frieda . . . cookin' your meals." (*Wedding Band*, 51)

Julia's words shake but do not crumble the racist foundation of the older
white woman. Parting with her son, Herman's mother issues the
irrefutable invective, "I'm as high over you as Mount Everest over the
sea. White reigns supreme. . . . I'm white, you can't change that"
(*Wedding Band*, 51).

Ensuing events, enacted in the lives of other backyard members, fore-
shadow the ultimate unmasking of reality between Herman and Julia.
First, Mattie laments to Lula and Julia that she cannot receive October's
allotment check because, counter to the impression she has given, she
and October are not legally married. She admits that a previous marriage to a man who physically abused her bars their legal union, since
the state disallows divorce. Next, a scheduled military parade intended
to honor all the soldiers going to war turns out to be a sham for Nelson,
since none of the black enlisted men shipping out can march with their
white counterparts. Because of their skin color, they must march at the
rear. Third, Lula recounts an incident in which she saved Nelson from a
life of imprisonment by pretending to be worthless and ignorant before
a white court. Julia is the last to confront her illusory vision as she realizes that Herman has never in the truest sense been "her-man." She fully
understands that it is not really Herman's mother who has controlled
their lives but Herman, who has permitted the control. Never actually
wanting to go to New York, Herman uses his debt to his mother as an
excuse for staying put. He has in fact chosen his bakery over Julia; own-
ing a business that satisfies his artistic impulse and need for self-actualization takes precedence over satisfying her emotional needs.

Herman's denial of Julia's blackness has likewise been a destabilizing
factor in their relationship. Inscribed in Herman's perception of Julia as
not being like other blacks is the belief that a definitive, repulsive black
blob does indeed exist. While he accepts her as an individual, he rejects
blacks as a people. Moreover, comparing the black experience with the
immigrant experience, Herman has never conceded her peculiar and distinct social position and struggle as an African American woman. Over
the years he has silenced her on issues of race: "the one thing" they
"never talk about," she accuses, is "white folks killin' me and mine. You
wouldn't let me speak" (*Wedding Band*, 62). That love does not conquer
all and that 10 years of interracial love cannot be divorced from centuries
of interracial hate are the realities to which Julia must accede.

Race over Sisterhood The racial tensions that exist between black women and white men, black and white men, and black women and black men subvert the play's core issue of interracial and intraracial sisterhood. The Bell Man, the poor, abrasive door-to-door salesman who enters the black women's community, is disrespectful, condescending, and exploitative. In a more equitable socioeconomic situation, he would be respectfully solicitous of the women's patronage, but because of the women's underclass status, he controls their commercial dependency on him. In an arrangement similar to the exploitative system of southern sharecropping, the buying-on-time trade that the Bell Man transacts will keep the women indebted to him on a variety of levels. Using the disrespectful familial names black women were called during slavery and afterward, he addresses them as "Aunty" and "Sister." He also violates their privacy by entering their homes uninvited. The sexualization of racism and the knowledge that Julia is intimately involved with a white man convince the Bell Man that she will be open to accommodating any white male sexually, him included. Her rejection of his noxious advances results in his calling her a "sick-minded bitch" (*Wedding Band,* 16) and attributing her dismissal of him to classism rather than to his utter unattractiveness and her complete lack of interest.

The Bell Man's emasculation of Nelson is no less racial and sexual and confines him to a nebulous liminality, "that 'betwixt and between' phase of rites of passage when an individual has left one fixed social status but has not yet been incorporated into another."[24] The denial by whites of his passage into manhood suspends him in limbo where he is neither man nor boy. Asserting his manhood, Nelson cautions the Bell Man to knock before entering his mother's house. The Bell Man's reply, a lynching threat—"Don't letcha uniform go to your head, Boy, or you'll end your days swingin' from a tree" (*Wedding Band,* 55)—illuminates the reality that an African American male, even one willing to die on foreign soil to protect his country, cannot protect his household on domestic soil. Marching at the end of a military parade in honor of soldiers being sent to the front and having whites throw a pail of dirty water on him while he is dressed in full military regalia exemplify the denigration that men of color in America have suffered. The white seal of approval is given only to Uncle Greenlee types, Uncle Toms who signify in the affairs of other blacks and ingratiate themselves to whites.

Lula's intervention in the conflict between her son and the salesman contains a pathetic irony: "Nelson, go on off to war 'fore somebody kills you" (*Wedding Band,* 55). The black man in white America, Childress demonstrates, is safer on the battlefield than in his own backyard. "What's hard" about serving his country, Nelson laments in his parting speech to his neighbors, "ain't the goin', it's the comin' back" (*Wedding Band*, 59). Neither Nelson nor October, when he returns, will be respected for his patriotism and rewarded with first-class citizenship.

The roles that the black woman plays in the maligning of the black male and the subverting of his manhood assume several configurations in *Wedding Band*. Childress frames scenes that address the black woman's verbal castigation of the black man, her attempt to make the black man a kept man, her complicity in keeping him from exercising his manhood, and the black man's charge that she violates racial exclusivity by sexually consorting with white men.

White-identified Fanny scorns the entire black race and castigates black men at every turn. When not deriding Lula's dead husband as "triflin'" or as "One nothin' piece-a man," she is justifying her maidenhood; no black man has "come up to [her] high standard" and "colored men don't know how to do nothin' right" (*Wedding Band*, 8, 54). "Plenty-a these hungry, jobless, bad-luck colored men, just-a itchin' to move in on my gravy-train. I don't want 'em," she boasts to Nelson at the same moment that she proposes providing for him if he reciprocates with marriage or consents to become her "business advisor," who "wouldn't have to step outside for a thing . . . food, fun and finance . . . all under one roof" (*Wedding Band*, 37). Fanny's interest lies in procuring companionship for herself, not empowering Nelson. Her offer to supply all of his needs is as repressive and emasculating as the white power structure's intent to deny them. Both militate against black male self-determination, self-actualization, and self-esteem.

Lula, who has reared Nelson in the absence of a father figure, has unconsciously conspired with the white dominant culture to suppress the manhood of her adoptive son. Curbing his racial anger and striving to keep Nelson from fighting against human injustices, Lula advocates passivity and acceptance. "It don't pay to get mad. . . . It's their country and their uniform, so just stay out the way," she counsels (*Wedding Band*, 11). Nelson is acutely aware that his mother derives reassurance from seeing him in the safe, subservient role of working for whites but becomes anxious when confronted with the possibility that he may act on dangerous self-expression. Lula is in the unenviable position of every African American mother of her day, whose responsibility to teach survival to her son in a racially hostile environment meant blunting "his masculine assertiveness and aggression lest these put the boy's life in jeopardy" when he interacts with whites.[25] The black mother's role in the development of her son's manhood is filled with contradictions. On the one hand, it is her maternal duty to encourage his development and expression of manhood, on the other, she must be the major inhibiting instrument of it.

Julia's liaison with Herman is emblematic of the betrayal black men perceive at the hands of attractive black women. Nelson, whose girl-friend has refused his proposal of marriage because, in view of his racial impotence, he has nothing to offer a black woman, resents Julia's accep-tance of "Massa" Herman, who after 10 years of common-law marriage, has offered her nothing. The knowledge of his lack of access to white women, along with his racial memory of the slavemaster's rape, concubi-nage, and sexual exploitation of black women, heightens Nelson's resentment of white males. Admonishing Julia to save any words she has for him as long as the white Herman lies ensconced in her bed, Nelson indicts her as a racial traitor and the giving of her body to a white man as an act of betrayal:

> They set us on fire 'bout their women. String us up, pour on kerosene and light a match. Wouldn't I make a bright flame in my new uniform? . . . I'm thinkin' 'bout black boys hangin' from trees in Little Mountain, Elloree, Winnsboro. . . . and *he's* got nothin' to offer. The one layin' on your mattress, not even if he's kind as you say. He got nothin' for you. . . . but some meat and gravy or a new petticoat . . . or maybe he can give you meriny-lookin' little bastard chirrun for us to take in and raise up. We're the ones who feed and raise 'em when it's like this . . . They don't want 'em. They only too glad to let us have their kin-folk. As it is, we supportin' half-a the slave-master's offspring right now. (*Wedding Band*, 41–42)

Of the many slave women who either sexually sacrificed their bodies for survival or prostituted themselves for material gain, Nelson clearly locates Julia as a contemporary paradigm of the latter group.

The ritualized transference of interracial resentment to the intraracial gender conflict, from male to female, informs the tension between Nelson and Julia. Reminding Nelson that he failed to retaliate against the whites who doused him with dirty water, Julia counters Nelson's accusations of racial sabotage by asserting that his attack of her via Herman is decentered. She challenges him to fight those who fight him, to assault those who are responsible for assaulting him, not those who are accessible to his rage yet are innocent of its provocation. Julia refuses to be the proverbial scapegoat, the black woman as "de mule uh de world," who, as Hurston's character Nanny in *Their Eyes Were Watching God* explains, allows the black man to dump on her what the white man loads upon her.[26]

Art, Absence of Men, and Difference Excepting race and class, the women in *Wedding Band* have personal similarities that could potentially serve as platforms for their unity rather than their discord. First, the majority of the women, combining utility and artistry, work creatively with their hands. Lula designs paper roses for funeral arrangements. Mattie makes candy to supplement the income she earns as a nanny. Julia, hired to do home sewing for a store, hand-finishes ladies' shirtwaists. Annabelle has a talent for playing the piano (although her mother's compulsion to use her talent as the means of improving her family's social status has diminished her interest). Second, all are single woman who have in some sense found it difficult to sustain nurturing relationships with men. In the cases of Julia, Mattie, and Annabelle, absent men shape lonely existences. Fanny, believing that no black man is good enough for her, has never married. She proposes to Nelson, who is half her age, but he declines. Both Lula, whose husband was unfaithful, and Herman's mother, whose husband drank and repulsed her sexually, are widows. Julia and Mattie are unable to legalize their common-law marriages of 10 and 11 years, respectively. Neither enjoys a man's name or his protection, since white patriarchal laws deprive them of access to divorce and marriage with the mate of their choice. Annabelle's excuse for delaying marriage to Walter, a sailor stationed in Brooklyn, parallels Julia's for still not being married to Herman. Annabelle's mother controls their lives. Because of her maternal control, neither daughter nor common-law daughter-in-law can flee north to marriage and self-determination. Last, all the women are under de jure and de facto limitations by virtue of their sex and/or race that restrict their movements as private citizens. In this fragmented, segregated community of women, each fails to identify self in other, rendering each insensitive to the plight and needs of other women and generating both intra- and interracial anger.

The backyard community of black women all share the same racial affiliation, the same racial history, and the same working class status, yet their perceptions of difference among them discourage true intraracial nurturance and sisterhood. Catherine Wiley comments on this lack of a unified sisterhood:

These characters who inhabit Miss Fanny's backyard tenement underscore the vexed issue of difference as explored by . . . feminist scholars. . . . Julia's problem throughout the play is less her white lover than her reluctance to see herself as a member of the black community. Although a mostly white theatre audience would see her as a different sort of heroine because of race, her black neighbors perceive her as different from them for issues more complex than skin color. She assumes that her racial transgression with Herman will make her unwelcome among the women she wishes to confide in, but her aloofness from their day-to-day interests also serves as a protective shield. . . . In this, Julia is similar to Lutie Johnson in Ann Petry's *The Street,* written in 1946. Both characters are ostensibly defined by their unequal relations with men, but their potential for salvation lies in the larger community that depends on the stability of its women. (Wiley, 188)

Prior to coming to the backyard community, Julia has lived an isolated existence in a black middle-class neighborhood that ostracized her because in all likelihood it viewed her as inferior. The instability with which someone of her standing—a woman living alone, presumably unmarried, who is shrouded in mystery—threatens the community is unacceptable. Conducting an illicit sexual liaison with a white man intensifies the threat she represents, solidifying her status as pariah. Thus, in the backyard, her aloofness and her neighbors' perception that she sees herself as superior to the underclass community exclude her from the women's community. Living without essence, Julia is caught in an existential dilemma. She is physically in the community but not spiritually a part of it. Her acceptance of Lula's invitation to a prayer gathering in the yard moments after she and Herman have exchanged anniversary gifts points to her need to belong, to connect to a greater whole than her present insular existence allows.

The same qualities that make Julia accessible to Herman render her inaccessible to the women of the yard. Her beauty, refinement, impressive attire, literacy, and financial independence evidence her as quality, as a lady. In contrast, Lula, Fanny, and Mattie, who have been called upon to wear the mask of subservient self-protection, must compromise any aspiration to refinement and ladyhood. Lula recounts to Julia an episode in which her dignity and ladylike behavior had to take a back seat to survival. To save Nelson from life in prison and the chain gang, she crawled and cried in front of a courtroom full of whites, "Please white folks, yall's everything, I'se nothing." Julia's response, "Oh, Miss Lula, a lady's not supposed to crawl and cry," draws Lula's pragmatic retort: "I was savin' his life" (*Wedding Band,* 57). Fanny, in like fashion, spontaneously assumes the humble servant role, deferring to the whites who enter onto her property. Apparently, Julia has not had to indulge whites at the expense of her dignity. Nor has she seemingly been faced with the reality that saving a life or preserving one's livelihood supersedes preserving one's ladyhood and dignity.

In breaching the black woman's expected code of unconditional loyalty to the black man by taking a white lover while recklessly violating whites' prohibition of racial mixing, Julia compounds her exclusion from the black female community. She fails to put race before the dictates of her gender and personal choice, and she refuses to don a mask of self-effacement, even to secure black security. Intraracial class distinctions keep the black women from attaining a viable sisterhood.

Julia's Liberating Anger The expression of repressed anger for having allowed her own oppression liberates Julia. Julia's angry exchange with Herman's mother activates her voice, crystallizes a realistic view of her 10-year relationship with Herman, and facilitates a communal nexus with the women of the yard. Herman's mother reminds Julia that no matter where she goes, her position as a black woman will remain unchanged. Fleeing to the North may lead to the changing of her last name if she marries Herman, but the racial ancestry she shares with the women of the yard and all African Americans are her permanent legacy. Julia has not worn the mask of self-effacement, but she has for love's sake voluntarily worn the mask of silence and abdicated control of her life. "As Julia assumes control, she discovers her 'voice' and she realizes that she need not fear to speak. Hers is a black woman's voice, shaped by history as she begins to make connections between her gender and her race. Childress makes quite clear that women should never fear their own voice; for the silence 'hurts.'"[27]

The removal of the chain and wedding band from her neck symbolizes her release from the shackles of her 10-year relationship with Herman and from her exile in a raceless, peopleless, liminal space. Presenting the wedding band on a chain to Mattie reconstitutes a new marriage and chain of connection to black women and men, from whom she has been socially divorced for too long:

JULIA: Surprise. Present.
MATTIE: For me?
JULIA: Northern tickets . . . and a wedding band.

MATTIE: I can't take that for nothing.
JULIA: You and Teeta are my people.
MATTIE: Yes.
JULIA: You and Teeta are my family. Be my family.
MATTIE: We your people whether we blood kin or not. (*Wedding Band,* 64)

Julia Augustine's odyssey figures an ascendance from community as an area of common living to *communitas,* the sharing of an emotional legacy and human bond.[28] The liberating physical journey that Julia has been eager to embark upon for the past 10 years is taken psychologically. Coming to terms with self means gaining access to communal space; Julia no longer needs to travel to the North or to yet another community to resolve her feelings of isolation.

The women of the backyard in *Wedding Band* depend increasingly on themselves and one another rather than on absent men. Childress's feminism in the play insists, as Marge Jennet Price-Hendricks posits, "that women . . . control their lives. Black women must confront those gender ideologies which have determined their existence. To be black and a woman in America means facing oppressive economic and social obstacles; racism and sexual exploitation are pervasive elements in her existence. However, to be black, a woman and without a woman's community is to be almost totally helpless in overcoming those obstacles" (194).

A continuing cycle of racism—even between black and white women—is evident in *Wedding Band,* but perhaps, as Childress's optimistic ending subtly hints, it will not necessarily be an eternal one. Among women from the old school of America's segregationist politics, the success in effecting an integrated women's cooperative and community will prove the most problematic and perhaps the most disappointing. Women like Herman's mother, carrying their own class baggage about self, are hardest to reach. Hatred of her own German ethnicity exacerbates her hatred of blacks. The shouting of racial and ethnic epithets—"Black, sassy nigger" and "Kraut, knuckle-eater, and red neck"—between Herman's mother and Julia (*Wedding Band,* 50) clouds the hope of relaxing the tensions between the next generation of black and white women, as represented by Teeta and Princess, the little white girl for whom Mattie serves as a nanny. In an earlier scene, the young girls have already made bigotry a part of their discourse in play. While the two jump rope they chant "Ching, ching, China-man eat dead rat . . . Knock him in the head with a baseball bat" (*Wedding Band,* 22). Even at her young age, Princess (as her name implies) expects verbal deference from her black playmate:

PRINCESS: You wanta jump?
TEETA: Yes.
PRINCESS: Say "Yes, Mam." (*Wedding Band,* 22–23)

Annabelle, the literal "sister" in the play, is the character who embodies hope for the future of interracial sisterhood (Wiley, 195). Though not without her faults, she has not—like her mother—been cut off from the potential to love. Disapproving of her brother's interracial relationship largely for selfish reasons—Herman will not marry Celestine and free her to marry Walter—she holds both Julia and Herman responsible for their 10-year affair and is willing peacefully to share her view. She tells Julia, "I'm sorry . . . so sorry it had to be this way. I can't leave with you thinkin' I uphold Herman, and blame you. I say a man is responsible for his own behavior" (*Wedding Band,* 49).

At the conclusion, Julia bars Annabelle, her mother, and Fanny from her house so that Herman may die peacefully in her arms. Yet after the others exit the stage, Annabelle remains, moving closer to the house to listen to Julia's final words to her brother. In her forward movement and quiet listening to Julia resides optimism for the future relationship between black and white women. Unlike her mother, whose racism provokes her to respond to Julia by engaging in a furious shouting match, Annabelle is open to what the black woman has to say.

As Catherine Wiley suggests, Julia's curtain speech directed to the dying Herman can also be applied to the two women remaining on stage. Annabelle's willingness to listen to Julia carries a deeper significance. Wiley maintains that because of Herman's impending death, Herman and Julia are not on their way to a smoother and easier existence, "but perhaps Julia and Annabelle will someday be on their way to mutual respect. . . . Sisterhood, especially from the point of view of white women learning to understand black women, begins with listening, not to what one wants to hear but to what is being said" (196).

Schizophrenia of Authorship

The anger Childress herself felt as a black female artist during her apprenticeship with the American Negro Theatre and in mainstream white theater is thinly veiled in the first phase of her writing. Reviewers of her canon accuse her of using her female characters as ideological mouthpieces, and indeed many of them function in varying degrees as her double, as extensions of her anxiety and rage at sexist and racist control in the theater and in life-at-large.

Throughout, Childress's art reflects her personal experience. Just like Florence, Childress withstood racist casting practices. Wiletta Mayer's challenge to the confinements of a racist script parallels Childress's challenge to the assertion that "in a play about Negroes and whites only a 'life and death thing' like lynching is interesting on stage" (Abramson, 189). Moreover, Childress quickly learned, like Wiletta, that the creativity she wanted to express through "theater" would be continually thwarted by "show business":

> I realized I had to have some other way of creating. I love acting, the art of acting, but not the business of acting and auditioning. Most of the time, I didn't like the parts they wanted me to play. . . . They were stereotypes, "packaged" situations. I don't necessarily mean derogatory stereotypes, but too predictable. "The black" would do one thing, "the white" another thing, and, of course, by the end they would all come together and resolve their differences—packaged solutions. (Betsko and Koenig, 67–68)

Childress's employment for a few months as a domestic in New York, coupled with the service work experiences of her Aunt Lorraine, served as emotional fuel and creative fodder for the exploits of the self-respecting Mildred Johnson. Childress authenticated the events of "The Health Card," "The Pocketbook Game," and "Mrs. James" as her own.

Under the cover of her characters, Childress resists the psychic disease of debilitating racism and the fallacy of sisterhood between black and white women. She, like her characters, exemplifies the thwarted black female artist engaged in psychological journey and evolution. And she, like they, constructively uses her indignation and anger to assert herself, liberating herself from a silence to which neither she nor her characters can continue to acquiesce.

Chapter Three

Blacks in the Abstract versus "Flesh and Blood Niggers": The Black Bourgeoisie, the Matriarchy, and Intraracial Conflict

The 1960s, a decade as much distinguished by black nonviolent protest, unity, and hope as by black militancy, divisiveness, and despair, drew Childress's artistic concentration away from the territory of interracial relationships and segregated sisterhood to the unfolding landscape of intraracial concerns. The rising black middle class, the relentless political activism of the civil rights movement, and the passage of the Civil Rights Act of 1964 and the Voting Rights Act of 1965 made transracial social, economic, political, and spatial equality seem less a dream and more an imminent reality. Yet as Houston A. Baker, Jr., observes, "[a]fter the beatings, arrests, bombings, and assassinations that comprised the white South's reaction to nonviolent, direct action protests by hundreds of thousands of civil rights workers from the late fifties to the mid-sixties, it was difficult for even the most committed optimist to feel that anything like AMERICA [that is, a raceless, classless, homogeneous nation] was an impending American social reality" (Baker, 71–72).

Disillusioned with the potential of nonviolence to effect an integrated egalitarianism, a militant young regime ushered in urban riots and the articulation of black power and nationalism and conceived a black aesthetic as part of its ideological platform. In place of submission to institutionalized Euro-American conventions, norms, and standards, black as beautiful, racial pride, negritude, and Africanism were stressed with the demand for political and social autonomy. The black arts movement, which Larry Neal called "the aesthetic and spiritual sister of the Black power concept," envisioned an art that spoke "directly to the needs and aspirations of Black America."

The literary current of the black consciousness movement in which Childress firmly grounded herself was radically different from the Harlem

Renaissance, which Larry Neal charged with failing "to address itself to
the mythology and life-styles of the Black community. . . . to take roots,
to link itself concretely to the struggles of that community, to become its
voice and spirit."[1] Along with other African American artists and aes-
theticians of the 1960s, Childress looked to the black masses as both subject and audience, as a source of both frustration and inspiration, as both
the cause of and the solution to issues profoundly affecting blackness.

"Whether playwrights of the 1960s fell into the category of real-
ism/naturalism, Marxism or structuralism," writes Mance Williams in his
study of the epoch, "the prevailing mood of the period was that of revolt,
outside and inside the theatre."[2] Under the directorship of Robert
Macbeth and the playwriting of Ed Bullins, the New Lafayette Theatre
committed itself to the production of plays by, about, and for blacks,
while a more radical, militant, revolutionary theater sprang to life under
the leadership of Imamu Amiri Baraka (LeRoi Jones). "Writers of this
revolutionary theatre," explains Elizabeth Brown-Guillory, "accuse
whites of persecuting or victimizing blacks but chastise blacks for facili-
tating their own victimization. Plays of this militant theatre generally
center on violent verbal and/or physical confrontation between blacks
and whites" (Brown-Guillory 1988, 27).

Years ahead of her contemporaries, Childress had already executed
revolts against the racism of the theater and black self-victimization in
Trouble in Mind (1955) and dismissed black dependency on white liberals
in the struggle for real political and economic equality in *Florence* (1949).
Instead of immersing her drama more completely in black-white physical and verbal confrontation, Childress, as the decade concluded, discon-
tinued interracial plots altogether. *Wedding Band* (1966) and *The World on
a Hill* (1968) represent her last treatments in the 1960s of white characters and white and black confrontation. Moreover, her earlier subtle
depictions of white-identified Fanny Johnson in *Wedding Band* and John
Nevins in *Trouble in Mind* anticipated the indictment of the black bourgeoisie and black self-victimization that emerges as a central motif in the
second phase of her writing career—the short interim of 1969 to 1970.

In contrast to the racially mixed and sometimes racially ambiguous
scripts of the late 1960s and early 1970s by Adrienne Kennedy, Barbara
Molette, and Sonia Sanchez, Childress confines her drama during this
next phase to black characters embroiled in black issues, to problems
created by blacks that only blacks can exorcise and solve. Written in
close succession, *String* (1969), *Wine in the Wilderness* (1969), and *Mojo: A
Black Love Story* (1970), all one-act plays, target blacks in need of libera-

tion from the influence of middle-class, white, and sexist values. The cross-class and cross-gender castings of these plays illuminate the ideological stratifications that often alienate middle-class blacks from their underclass counterparts and that strain intimate relationships between black men and women.

The Black Bourgeoisie

Childress's censorious portraits of the misguided interests and antiblack attitudes of the status-conscious black bourgeoisie complement the scathingly critical study of the class that sociologist E. Franklin Frazier published in 1957, a little more than a decade earlier:

> The single factor that has dominated the mental outlook of the black bourgeoisie has been its obsession with the struggle for status. The struggle for status has expressed itself mainly in the emphasis upon "social" life or "society."
>
> . . . .
>
> Moreover, the black bourgeoisie have shown no interest in the "liberation" of Negroes except as it affected their own status or acceptance by the white community. They viewed with scorn the Garvey Movement with its nationalistic aims. They showed practically no interest in the Negro Renaissance. They wanted to forget the Negro's past, and they have attempted to conform to the behavior and values of the white community in the most minute details. Therefore they have often become, as has been observed, "exaggerated" Americans.
>
> Because of its struggle to gain acceptance by whites, the black bourgeoisie has failed to play the role of a responsible elite in the Negro community.[3]

Defined very broadly in socioeconomic terms, the black middle class ranged from craftsmen and clerks to professionals but was primarily constituted of educated blacks who derived their income principally from the services they rendered as white collar workers. Neither accepted by middle-class whites nor accepting of poor blacks, the black bourgeoisie segregated itself from members of their race who did not fall within their socioeconomic parameters.

Criticizing classist segregation and prejudice, Childress's plays of the late 1960s strike at the heart of bourgeois blacks' subscription to the idea of whiteness as an idealized, privileged natural state. Her denunciation of the prosperous blacks who emulate whites to gain white recognition and acceptance and her enunciation of the need for racial solidarity and cultural integrity echo the goal of the black consciousness movement: that black men and women aspire to blackness, idealizing themselves as black.

The Matriarchy

While challenging intraracial classist values and black self-hatred, Childress questions the true liberationist ethos of a political movement committed to a gender-biased ideology. The glorification of subservient, objectified, glamorized black womanhood and the demonization of the domineering black matriarch, albeit a theoretical classification, bespoke the aim of the black movement in the 1960s to create an acceptable sphere for black women paralleling that conventionally occupied by white women. For many supporters of the movement, black women were merely enabling pawns for the cause, not in need of political or social liberation themselves.

Exploding the myth of the emasculating and masculinized black matriarchy at a time when it was rapidly solidifying proved to be an arduous task. As Childress wrote in 1966, the "Negro woman has almost been omitted as important subject matter in the general popular American drama, television, motion pictures and radio." Yet when she is included it is "pointed out that she is too militant, so domineering, so aggressive, with son, husband, and brother, that it is *one* of the chief reasons for any unexpressed manhood on the part of the black man in America" ("Woman Playwright," 75; emphasis added). Childress rationalizes that "there must be some truth in this charge" when we consider the mother in James Baldwin's *Amen Corner* (1965), who "attempts to restrict her son and husband to her passive and withdrawn way of life." Two other dramatic examples she cites are the loving mother in Lorraine Hansberry's *A Raisin in the Sun* (1959), who "so dominates the home that she restricts her children and infringes upon the rights of her son as a man"; and the black mother in Louis Peterson's *Take a Giant Step* (1953), "who tries to separate her son from his black heritage in order to shield him from the realities of life" ("Woman Playwright," 75).

Even she, Childress admits, has created the "strong matriarchal figure," first in *Florence* and again in *Trouble in Mind,* but she is nonetheless disturbed by the expanding, unsubstantiated definition of the controversial black female image. Childress writes: "But now we frequently hear that strength has taken femininity away from her with the end result that she is *the* main culprit in any lack of expressed black manhood, and that she has been masculinized in the process. Certainly this is too easy and too misleading a conclusion" ("Woman Playwright," 75; emphasis added).

Many black men supporting the black consciousness movement not infrequently relegated the black woman to the status of either insignificant or matriarchal. Detailing the statistical evidence of black-female-headed households but providing little empirical psychological data to support the concept of a matriarchy, Daniel P. Moynihan's infamous report, "The Negro Family" (1965), laid the cornerstone for the myth of the black matriarch.[4] Theoretically, the black matriarchy originates with the black women who headed households in the absence of husbands for themselves and fathers for their children. The concept curiously implies that even when a black husband/father is present, the wife/mother remains the dominant member of the household. The myth was often plied in backlash against women who rejected the idea of a male-first movement or who were viewed as domineering threats to black manhood. "Castrating bitch" and "matriarch" became familiar castigating labels for women who asked why the search for black manhood should take precedence over the search for black womanhood.

Childress directly discounts the characterization of black women who have had to rely solely on themselves for physical, emotional, and economic survival as matriarchal, masculinized figures. She argues that implicit in the myth, which credits the black woman with dictatorial familial power, is the contradiction that the majority of black women, at the bottom rung of power, "didn't have nothin' to rule over, not a pot nor a window."[5] A cruel misnomer, declares bell hooks, "the term matriarch implies the existence of a social order in which women exercise social and political power, a state which in no way resembles the condition of black women or all women in American society" (hooks, 72). Childress exorcises this myth about black women that members of both sexes and races have so frequently invoked that they have come to regard it as sociohistorical truth.

String

String, a very free adaptation of Guy de Maupassant's "The Piece of String," a late nineteenth-century short story about a "gentle man—abused by vulgarians," captures the essence but changes the thematic focus of the original tale. De Maupassant's conclusion underscores the tragic effect of character assassination on an honest citizen. De

Maupassant's economical Norman peasant Mâitre Hauchecorne of Bréauté's insistent claim of hastily picking up a piece of string on the way to the market and not a lost leather pocketbook containing 500 francs goes unbelieved by the people of Goderville when Mâitre Malandain, his enemy, testifies that he saw him pick up the pocketbook. Despite the later return of the pocketbook by Marius Paumelle, Hauchecorne never recovers from the accusation of theft. Stricken by the injustice of the suspicion that he is somehow mixed up in the affair, he dies, deliriously proclaiming his innocence, reiterating: "a piece of string, a piece of string."[6] Childress shifts the focus to emphasize the dehumanizing toll class prejudice takes on the economically disadvantaged individual whom middle-class society judges on his appearance—what he owns and wears—instead of on his inner reality—his moral values.

Old Joe, a poor, rough-looking 55-year-old member of a New York City community who lives by salvaging discarded items, is Childress's Hauchecorne. A social gathering, a neighborhood association picnic on a summer Sunday in 1968, provides the setting. Mrs. Beverly, a civic-minded woman wearing a splashy outfit and fancy high-heeled shoes, enters the picnic area carrying a basket and other picnic paraphernalia. Mrs. Rogers, given to arrogant manners and wearing a well-cut linen suit with spectator pumps, enters closely behind her. Gossiping, the ladies agree that Maydelle, the picnic chairwoman, should be impeached and that Joe, whom they have labeled a social pariah, should be excluded from the neighborhood gathering. Seeking out their company after other groups of picnickers have banished him from theirs, Joe enters. The women, using items from the basket, occupy every possible seat Joe might take, including a rock and a tree stump, to prevent him from sitting down and socializing with them.

Following Joe, Maydelle enters, apologizing for the ill-treatment he received from yet someone else, L. V. Craig, the owner of a bar and grill. Craig enters, continuing his castigation of Joe and offering to buy from Mrs. Beverly the meat pies that she has made to sell to the group. He cannot, however, pay her right away because the denominations of the bills in his wallet are too large. Untying the package of meat pies, Mrs. Beverly drops the string used to bind it, and Joe, a collector of cast-off objects, surreptitiously picks it up and places it in his pocket when he believes no one is looking. Mrs. Beverly, however, notices his movements but cannot identify the object he conceals.

It is then that Craig discovers that his wallet containing $350 is missing. With the exception of Maydelle, the group accuses Joe of concealing the wallet despite his protestation that he only picked up Mrs. Beverly's discarded piece of string. While the others are off searching for the missing wallet, Katy, a young picnicker, returns the wallet but under a cloud of doubt and suspicion that Joe is somehow responsible for its earlier disappearance and now its sudden return. Craig insinuates to Joe, "One finds and the other reports. One is a full-grown, rusty man . . . the other is a baby child. Tell it any way you want but you mixed up in it."[7]

After Craig, Beverly, and Rogers depart, Maydelle expresses to Joe her renewed faith in his honesty: "I'm proud and glad that you gave it back. You've justified my faith . . . I'm proud because you couldn't steal. You just couldn't . . . even if you wanted to . . . you couldn't." Shattered by the implication that she believes he did steal the wallet before giving it back, Joe grabs a thermos bottle from the picnic table and threatens Maydelle: "I'll beat your damn brains out! Say you believe me! Say it or I'll kill you." Fearing for her safety, Maydelle acquiesces, "I believe you . . . I believe it was string . . . a piece of string . . . there! There! It was string. And don't you ever speak to me again for as long as you live." As she exits, Joe, in imitation of de Maupassant's Hauchecorne, reiterates his innocence—"String . . . string . . . a piece-a string . . . it was a piece-a string . . . string . . . string . . . a piece-a string"—as he slumps to the ground and the lights dim (String, 49).

"Ill-Assorted" People The black bourgeoisie in String fall neatly within Frazier's socioeconomic parameters. The wife of a government postal worker, Mrs. Rogers has claim to middle-class status. An entrepreneur, L. V. Craig, owns a prosperous bar and grill. Maydelle has a full-time job and the means to extend her education by attending night classes. Mrs. Beverly, a widow from the West Indies having difficulty making ends meet, projects a middle-class appearance through her dress and association with Mrs. Rogers. Each of these individuals exemplifies some degree of class consciousness and snobbery, while each exhibits his or her own peculiar brand of black self-hatred and antiliberationism.

Violating the conventional notions of picnic aesthetics, the formal dress and narrow opinions of Mrs. Rogers and to a lesser degree Mrs. Beverly classify them as upwardly mobile, status-conscious blacks. The women, wearing high-heeled shoes and fine attire, distinguish themselves from Joe, a wearer of odds and ends of cast-off clothing, who represents the underclass black they consider out of their social league and an embarrassment to the race.

A separatist, Mrs. Rogers expresses herself mainly in the attention she gives to "social" life or "society." She complains that the "block association is suddenly becoming over-crowded with the crass and the crude," that is, by people such as indigent Joe and intemperate Craig, whose business, as she categorizes it, is "third rate" (*String,* 29). "Weary of togetherness" with blacks from disparate social classes, she philoso-phizes that "in order to have a pleasant day you have to have people on the same level" (*String,* 29, 30). Otherwise, a gathering of economical-ly stratified blacks might be mistaken for a riot. Her judgment that "ill-assorted" people should not socialize harks back to the pronounce-ment of Herman's mother in *Wedding Band* that the mismatched, whether they be things or people, do not belong together (*Wedding Band,* 48).

To exorcise any impulsive self-expression that smacks remotely of blackness, Mrs. Rogers disparages any behavior by her race that does not conform to white formal standards in the most minute detail. To a loud burst of laughter in the distance, she responds, "Loud, loud, loud . . . too loud" (*String,* 27). What she truly means is "black, black, black . . . too black." Her ethnic censure and stereotyping overtly display themselves in her offensive inference that racial genetics is responsible for the adept-ness of West Indians, like Jews, in money matters.

The first in a series of insensitive male figures depicted in this phase of Childress's career, L. V. Craig gains the respect and envy of other blacks through conspicuous consumption. An egotist, the black businessman of the community flaunts his material possessions and his indifference to black suffering as well as liberation and empowerment. Buying all of Mrs. Beverly's meat pies, driving a Cadillac, and flashing a wallet full of money infuse him with a sense of importance. A big voice that crowds others out, he equates Joe's failed manhood with the absence of money. Emotionally unaffected by the economic vulnerability of Mrs. Beverly, poor Joe, and other struggling blacks, he ridicules prayer, protest, and penny-pinching as means of effecting change in their lives. "I don't do much cryin' though. No cryin', no marchin', no prayin' . . . L. V. Craig's gon' git his if there's any gittin to git. Pinchin' and prayin', scrimpin' and scufflin' . . . for somebody else not me . . . ain' for me," he pompous-ly boasts (*String,* 34).

Mocking black hope and protest, Craig condescendingly suggests that for amusement the group should sing "We Shall Overcome," the inspirational anthem of the civil rights movement. The rugged individu-alism and "pull yourself up by your bootstraps" philosophy he espouses are undercut by his willingness to exploit the people of his community for personal gain. Watering down the whisky he serves is one example of his egocentric ethics. The "manly" advice he gives to Joe after Katy returns his wallet is another: "You know one thing, man? Now that I got my bread back . . . I tell you this much. If I took somethin' I sure in hell would keep it. Don't never chicken out! Big enough to do it . . . go on and see it through" (*String*, 47). The statement sums up Craig's rationale for ruthlessly exploiting the black community.

Clothes Make the Man In Childress's drama the insincere support of the white-identified bourgeois black is just as debilitating to black racial pride and esteem as the well-meaning but oftentimes obstructive behavior of the white liberal. Maydelle has good intentions, but her support of Joe is as superficial as the advice she gives him to absolve himself of suspicion and to preserve his honor. The best advice she can summon to his aid is to alter his "looks" in order to alter the appearance of his guilt. Instead of firmly maintaining his honesty, she seeks to engineer its appearance. "If you had a nice suit," she comments, "perhaps none of this would have happened" (*String*, 44). Maydelle relies on the efficacy of façades, masks, and special effects; to wear the mask of respectability by physically clothing oneself with good character is all one needs to be perceived as trustworthy and respectable. Maydelle's contradictory message is that it is not what Joe is morally that counts but what people think he is. Joe knows, however, that looks are deceiving and that "puttin' on airs folk" are not necessarily honest folk:

JOE: L.V. got a nice suit, he got maybe forty nice suits and he live in a pretty white house with a lawn in the front of it . . . but he cheats . . . he puts water in the whiskey . . . that's stealin' . . . thou shalt not covet . . .

MAYDELLE: But he doesn't *look* like a thief, and that's very important.

JOE: What does a thief look like?

MAYDELLE: If you don't try to change your ways and be a little like other people it's going to go very hard for you. After all, they can't do all the changing in order to accommodate you. Why can't you realize that? (*String*, 44)

Implicit in her argument is the inference that Joe *looks* like a thief; ergo, the morality and ethics of an individual can be surmised by his clothes. Paradoxically, the others, whose clothing ensures their acceptance, respectability, and humanity—despite their actions to the contrary—are beyond reproach. Feigning sympathetic acceptance, Maydelle plays peace weaver but is just as bigoted as Craig, Rogers, and Beverly.

Outwardly she professes an unwavering confidence in the downtrodden Joe, but inwardly she believes as strongly in his guilt as the others.

The responsibility of the individual to conform to the community versus the responsibility of the community to accept the nonconformist who poses no threat to its stability and whose only crime is difference composes the play's subtextual tension. Because of his neighbors' class bias, Joe is doggedly harassed, but it is he who is expected to change to accommodate their bias. In Maydelle's estimation, the block belongs to the others and herself "but not as much" to Joe (*String,* 44); therefore, she authorizes only his partial occupation of a communal space that in fact wholly belongs to him. To accommodate Joe to the others, in addition to pressing for the upgrading of his clothing, she aims to silence him. "Be quiet, the quieter the better," she affirms.

Bearing no concrete proof of his guilt, all are willing to convict Joe on circumstantial evidence. His stooping to pick up an unidentified object is, as proof of his dishonesty, subordinate to his physical appearance and underclass status. The antagonistic socioeconomic milieu that entangles Joe bears a strong parallel to Eugene O'Neill's hostile social construction in *The Hairy Ape* (1922). Those belonging and aspiring to belong to the middle class, like those of the capitalist class who exploit the proletarian protagonist of O'Neill's drama, yank Joe about, beating him down to show their contempt for him. The group does violence to his personhood, crushing his dignity, honor, and last vestige of humanity. Reduced to his baser instincts for survival and self-protection, Joe strikes out, unwittingly becoming a victimizer as well as the victimized.

Wine in the Wilderness

In *Wine in the Wilderness,* Childress makes the point that the intersections of "sexism, racism, and classism are immutably connected to black women's oppression while making it crystal clear that black women triumph because of a strong spirit of survival inextricably linked to an African heritage" (Brown-Guillory 1990, 106). Enlisting the background of a Harlem riot as a controlling metaphor for communal and intraracial fragmentation, Childress foregrounds the underclass, undereducated heroine of *Wine in the Wilderness* as the true Africentrist, proud of blacks and her blackness. She stands in stark relief to bourgeois, intellectual blacks whose white assimilationist and classist values expose their racial disingenuousness. Espousing the in-vogue black power rhetoric of brotherhood, liberation, and nationalism, the middle-class antagonists of the play accessorize themselves with the trappings of African culture—the dashiki, the Afro hairstyle, and African objets d'art. But they relegate the black woman in the black movement to the same position assigned her by real-life activists like Stokely Carmichael: "prone."

The play's gender conflict exposes the black consciousness movement's ambition to establish a black male hegemony that replicated the gender and class biases of white patriarchy. The female protagonist of *Wine in the Wilderness* refutes the accusation that she is the product of a matriarchal society that has appropriated the manhood of the black male. Resistant to exploitation by pretentious middle-class blacks, she rejects the sexist prescriptions of passivity, submissiveness, voicelessness, and domesticity. An African ancestral connectedness, which the other black characters have failed to cultivate or have lost, enables her to resurrect a guiding, affirming blackness in the middle-class blacks she encounters. As Elizabeth Brown-Guillory posits, the female protagonist of *Wine in the Wilderness* is "a very spiritual and spirited woman," who "rises to serve as a healer to her wounded community whose psyche is in need of re-Africanization" (Brown-Guillory 1990, 108).

Childress situates the action of *Wine in the Wilderness* at the conclusion of a Harlem riot during the summer of 1964. Waiting out the storm of street violence in his apartment, Bill Jameson, a 33-year-old painter, receives a telephone call from his neighbors Sonny-man, a writer, and Sonny-man's wife, Cynthia, a social worker. They announce that they have found the perfect model for Bill's work-in-progress, the third panel of a triptych dedicated to the theme of black womanhood.

Before they arrive, Bill describes the triptych to Oldtimer, a homeless man, who drops by with loot picked up off the street. The first panel, titled "Black Girlhood," depicts innocence—"a charming little girl in Sunday dress and hair ribbon." The second reveals "a beautiful woman" with "deep mahogany complexion" who is "cold but utter perfection, draped in startling colors of African material." She is, Bill states, "'Wine in the Wilderness' . . . Mother Africa, regal, black womanhood in her noblest form." He explains that the third canvas, now blank, will contain the image of "the kinda chick that is grass roots, . . . no, . . . underneath the grass. The lost woman, . . . what the society has made out of our women. She's as far from my African queen as a woman can get and still be female. She's ignorant, unfeminine, coarse, rude . . . vulgar . . . there's no hope for her. . . . If you had to sum her up in one word it would be nothin'!" (*Wine,* 125–26).

Wearing a wig and mismatched skirt and sweater, 30-year-old Tomorrow Marie Fields, called Tommy, arrives with Sonny-man and Cynthia under the impression that the two are trying to match her up romantically with Bill. Lacking the sophistication and college education of the others, Tommy, an eighth-grade dropout, is unpretentious, good-natured, and polite. When the men leave to get the Chinese food Bill promises Tommy in exchange for posing, Tommy shares with Cynthia her attraction to Bill. Cynthia attempts to discourage Tommy's affection, warning that Bill's art comes first and that she should not put her trust in men. Tommy, however, understands Cynthia's true message, that she is "aimin' too high by looking at Bill" (*Wine*, 133).

Seeking honesty, she asks Cynthia to tell her why men like Bill fail to find her attractive. Cynthia explains, stating "You're too brash. You're too used to looking out for yourself. It makes us lose our femininity. . . . It makes us hard. . . . You have to let the black man have his manhood again. You have to give it back, Tommy. . . . Don't chase him. . . . Let him pursue you. . . . Let him do the talking. Learn to listen. Stay in the background a little. Ask his opinion . . . 'What do you think, Bill?'. . . What we need is a little more sex appeal" (*Wine*, 134–35). Wearing an Afro herself, she recommends that Tommy not wear a wig. The conversation between the women terminates with the return of the men. Oldtimer, Cynthia, and Sonny-man leave so that Bill can commence painting.

Admitting her ignorance about books, Tommy encourages Bill to share his knowledge of black history. In between his elaborations on Frederick Douglass and Monroe Trotter, he criticizes black women in general and Tommy in particular. Uncomfortable about her shabby clothing, Tommy suggests that he paint her another time. His insistence that she keep on the wig for the portrait vexes her, and she accidentally spills orange drink on herself. Perturbed by her clumsiness, Bill gives her an African wrap in which to change while he talks on the phone.

Tommy overhears Bill describing to the caller the ebony queen of the "Wine in the Wilderness" panel and mistakenly thinks he is describing her. "You just make sure your exhibition room is big enough to hold the crowds that's gonna congregate to see this fine chick I got here. . . . an ebony queen of the universe. . . . but best of all and most important. . . . She's tomorrow . . . she's my tomorrow," he states (*Wine*, 140–41). Feeling valued and possibly loved, Tommy, sans wig, emerges relaxed, confident, and beautifully draped. She sits on the model stand, reciting bits of her family history as conversation. Astonished by her radical physical transformation, Bill is strongly attracted to this Tommy. Unable to reconcile her present appearance with the earlier one, he loses his incentive to paint. The two grow closer, embrace, kiss, and ultimately spend the night together.

The next morning, an elated Tommy is deflated and angered when Oldtimer returns and inadvertently reveals that she is not the African queen but the "messed-up chick" of the triptych. Sonny-man and Cynthia arrive shortly thereafter, and Tommy denounces them all, accusing them of spouting pro-black rhetoric when in actuality they obviously despise "flesh and blood niggers" (*Wine,* 146), as evidenced by their classist, sexist, and deceptive treatment of her. Bill's consciousness is slow to be raised, but her insight takes the artist beyond his limited perception, inspiring him to begin the triptych anew. The "chick" of the old triptych, "a dream I drummed up outta the junk room of my mind," was painted "in the dark" with "all head and no heart. I couldn't see until you came," Bill pleads (*Wine,* 149).

The first panel of the re-visioned triptych will depict Oldtimer as emblematic of the black man's past, when he was denied access to education, unions, and factory work. The second panel will contain Sonny-man and Cynthia, representative of the "Young Man and Woman working together to do our thing." Bill persuades Tommy to pose for the center panel, the woman of the future, the "Wine in the Wilderness" woman, who has come "through the biggest riot of all, . . . somethin' called 'Slavery,' and she's even comin' through the 'now' scene" (*Wine,* 149). As the black woman whose identity is clearly etched as survivor, Tommy will be the inspiration for the black men and women of tomorrow.

Cultural Symbol versus Cultural Substance The setting of the play, Bill Jameson's partially renovated Harlem apartment, is conspicuously dominated by cultural iconography. African sculpture, wall hangings, paintings, and books on African American history signify the occupant's fashionable but vacuous preoccupation with African artifacts. An array of multicultural icons—a Chinese Buddha incense-burner, a Native American feather war helmet, a West Indian travel poster, a Mexican serape, and a Japanese fan—further objectifies Bill's vapid efforts to proclaim a political kinship with other oppressed people of color. He cannot sympathetically or psychically relate to those other cultures represented in his apartment, however, because he has failed to connect wholly with his own.

A creation of elitist, black, middle-class culture in imitation of white patriarchy, Bill is more concerned with cultural symbols than with cultural substance. The most telling indicator of his cultural insubstantiality is the exotic cluster of African symbols and associations he attaches to his vision of "Wine in the Wilderness," perfect black womanhood. The exotic "cold" image of the ebony queen of the universe, of the "Sudan, the Congo River, the Egyptian Pyramids," in essence Mother Africa who "has come through everything that has been put on her" (*Wine,* 125, 140), bears no resemblance to flesh and blood African and African American women who have actually withstood the trials and tribulations of daily struggle and survival. His "gorgeous satin chick," whom every man would "most like to meet on a desert island, or around the corner from anywhere" (*Wine,* 141), panders to male fantasy.

Bill's misguided vision of "Wine in the Wilderness" is the Madison Avenue paradigm of physical female beauty, only in blackface. His queen is the slick, air-brushed, glamorized, ornamental woman who mutely stares from billboards and magazine advertisements. With her blackness defamiliarized in a traditional white imaging of beauty, she propagates the ideology of whiteness, not blackness. Antithetical to the struggling black woman in America, the woman on the canvas is nothing but accessories—"startling colors of African material" and "golden headdress sparkling with brilliants and sequins . . . [s]omethin' you add on or take off" (*Wine,* 125, 148). Flawless in appearance and conceptualization, Bill's "Wine in the Wilderness" has no grounding in reality.

Mainstream Assimilation　Because of their assimilation of mainstream values, Bill and his neighbors, Sonny-man and Cynthia, more concerned with black symbols, black discourse, and blackness in the abstract than in the concrete, disassociate themselves from blacks of lower socioeconomic status. Their classist disrespect for Oldtimer, who represents age, experience, and their ancestral past, exemplifies their detachment. In all the time they have known Oldtimer, never have they been genuinely interested enough to ask him his real name. His serving as their court fool and as an up-close example of how politically untogether poor, uneducated blacks can be, has militated against their recognition of his personhood. Similarly, the trio is interested in Tommy for her symbolic value, not for her real self. Voicing both class and regional bias, they view her as "the kinda woman that grates on your damn nerves . . . back-country . . . right outta the wilds of Mississippi," though she was born and reared in Harlem (*Wine,* 126). Since she "ain't fit for nothin'" and "there's no hope for her," political enlightenment and social empowerment are, theoretically, wasted on her. The only sensible response from privileged, enlightened blacks like themselves is "to . . . just pass her by" (*Wine*, 126).

Living in Harlem, a mecca of blackness, yet not identifying with their black sisters and brothers on the street, has severed the middle-class blacks of the play from their racial roots. Tommy forces them to face their intraracial bigotry and their illusion that they are different from "the black masses" when she comprehends that they see her as inferior:

SONNY-MAN: The sister is upset.
TOMMY: And you stop callin' me "the" sister, . . . if you feelin' so brotherly why don't you say "my" sister? Ain't no we-ness in your talk. "The" Afro-American, "the" black man, there's no we-ness in you. Who you think you are?
SONNY-MAN: I was talkin' in general er . . . my sister, 'bout the masses.
TOMMY: There he go again. "The" masses. Tryin' to make out like we pitiful and you got it made. You the masses your damn self and don't even know it. (*Wine*, 147)

Tommy reminds them that the white definition of "nigger" extends equally to them: "When they say 'nigger', just dry-long so, they mean educated you and uneducated me" (*Wine*, 147–48). Her words startle Bill into a psychological journey toward black affirmation. Shocked, he discovers that counter to what he has been taught, the dictionary def-inition of "nigger" does not mean "a low, degraded person" but "A Negro . . . A member of any dark-skinned people" (*Wine*, 147). Tommy's definition of "nigger"—by which she designates both the rioters who have burned her out of her apartment and Bill, once she discovers he has misrepresented his intentions in painting her—applies to those blacks who hurt and exploit other blacks to fuel their own self-esteem and to satisfy their own egocentric aims.

The racial denial, divisiveness, and do-nothing politics of Bill and other bourgeois blacks are just as destructive to black advancement and self-acceptance as the looting and burning done by those who destroy their own people's businesses and homes in the name of revo-lution or as the scavenging of those who profit from the leavings. The rioters, as Tommy points out, holler "whitey, whitey . . . but who they burn out? Me" (*Wine*, 130). Their violence is not unleashed on those they regard as the enemy but internalized, deflected onto the black community.

Contemptuous of black Harlemites, Bill, like the rioters, ironically abuses his own people, thereby revealing his unrecognized self-hatred and self-devaluation. Quick to sermonize but lacking a plan of his own, Bill is critical of both black factionalism—the rioters and looters—and black unity—the leaderships of Malcolm X and Martin Luther King, Jr. Nothing blacks do seems to please him. Even his suburban upbringing in Jamaica, Long Island, where everyone in his family worked for the post office and every house on his block had "an aluminum screen door with a duck on it," receives his disdain (*Wine*, 142). Tommy plainly points all this out to him, perceiving that his rejection of her symbolizes his rejection of his mother, his family, the "flesh and blood" black community:

> Ain't a-one-a us you like that's alive and walkin' by you on the street . . . you don't like flesh and blood niggers. . . . If a black somebody is in a history book, or printed on a pitcher, or drawed on a paintin' . . . or if they're a statue, . . . dead, and outta the way, and can't talk back, then you dig 'em and full-a so much-a damn admiration and talk 'bout "our" history. But when you run into us livin' and breathin' ones, with the life's blood still pumpin' through us, . . . then you comin' on 'bout we ain' never together. You hate us, that's what! You hate black me! . . .
>
> Maybe I look too much like the mother that give birth to you. Like the Ma and Pa that worked in the post office to buy you a house and a screen door with a damn duck on it. And you so ungrateful you didn't even like it . . . You didn't like who was livin' behind them screen doors. Phoney Nigger! (*Wine*, 146–47)

Even with limited education and social exposure, Tommy knows that identity and self-worth do not come from acting out prescriptive black roles, reading black history, surrounding oneself with African art, or holding one's familial roots in contempt.

A Guiding Africentrism Essential to the sustenance of a positive black national culture, Childress argues, is the possession of a guiding respectful Africentrism. The nurturing racial attitudes that Tommy embraces serve as the essential ingredients for the propagation of that culture. Unlike Bill and his bourgeois neighbors, Tommy responds to Oldtimer, her elder and a survivor of past black oppression, as an equal.

Her caring acknowledgment of his identity as Edmond L. Matthews recovers his personhood and reclaims his rightful membership in the social framework from which the others have consistently excluded him.

Tommy does not assume she "knows" Oldtimer by reading his physical appearance as a sociopsychological text. She respectfully tells him, "I'll call you Oldtimer like the rest but I like to know who I'm meetin'" (*Wine*, 128). The others have narrowly defined Matthews by what he is, not by who he is, while the who of his identity, as Tommy intuitively comprehends, is more important than the what. Her humanity toward Oldtimer is again demonstrated near the end of the play when he debases himself because of his intellectual deficiency. Tommy, gently rebuking his self-deprecation, remarks, "Hush that talk . . . You know lotsa things, everybody does" (*Wine*, 144).

Tommy's respectful regard for the intimate relationships between black men and women is apparent from the moment she enters Bill's apartment. Thirty and unmarried, she desires male intimacy and commitment; nevertheless, she is unwilling to sabotage the committed relationship of another black woman with a man in her own pursuit of love and companionship. For the benefit of any significant other possibly present in Bill's apartment, Tommy makes it clear that she will have nothing to do with a married or attached man. Speaking loudly, she asserts, "Let's get somethin' straight. I didn't come bustin' in on the party, . . . I was asked. If you married and any wives or girl-friends round here . . . I'm innocent" (*Wine*, 129). Later, when she concerns herself more with the benefits that marriage and a family will confer on her individually rather than on the race as a whole, she seems uncomfortable. Implicit in her apology to Bill that both "might be good; for your people as a race, but I was thinkin' 'bout myself a little," is the belief that considering herself first is a bit selfish (*Wine*, 138).

Her familial and ancestral pasts empower Tommy. Unlike Bill, who is contemptuous of his parents and suburban upbringing, Tommy uses her now-deceased mother, a victim of spousal abandonment and its all too often ensuing cycle of poverty, as a major motivation for taking control of her life. Observing her mother "tyin' up her stockin's with strips-a rag 'cause she didn't have no garters" and having herself had "[n]othin' much" to eat when she returned home from school induced Tommy to seek employment and self-determination (*Wine*, 133). She is not resentful that she had to terminate her schooling and does not blame her mother for their impoverished circumstances.

Tommy's account of her family history further demonstrates her racial groundedness. In contrast to Bill's detachment from the black community and black history, Tommy is closely attached to her home-town's ordinary, local people, often members of her own family, and their small but real accomplishments—winning a scholarship in a speech contest, for instance, or tracing the family history back to slaves from Sweetwater Springs, Virginia. Reciting the geneses of The Improved Benevolent Protective Order of Elks of the World and the African Methodist Episcopal Zion Church in which she taught for two years identifies her as an active bearer of oral tradition and preserver of her cultural heritage.

Directing no hatred toward whites, Tommy's Africentrism is not predicated on racism; she simply prefers the company of blacks. Presented with the choice of a live-in domestic job on Park Avenue with her own private bath and television and work in a Harlem dress factory among her friends, she chooses the latter. In contrast to Cynthia, who attempted to date white men but gave up when she realized that her education would not ensure her passage into the "so called 'integrated' world," Tommy affirms that she has never been interested in white men and doesn't find them physically attractive. "When I look at 'em," she tell Cynthia, "nothin' happens . . . . I don't hate 'em, don't love 'em, . . . just nothin' shakes a-tall" (*Wine,* 134).

The Matriarchal Society Cynthia, who is unable to shrug off the oppressive patriarchy of the movement and defines herself in contrast to the image of the black matriarch, perceives herself as the responsible black woman who willingly subjugates her autonomy, spirit, and vision to help establish a black patriarchal world order (Price-Hendricks, 197). Accepting the commands and chastisement of her husband, she is at his beck and call. Sonny-man's directive that she run down to their apart-ment and perform the gender-specific activity of cooking eggs for Bill's model draws from her a "weary look" but a complacent verbal response: "Oh, Sonny, that's such a lovely idea" (*Wine,* 131). Later, she is rendered mute by Sonny-man's childlike chiding of her for apologizing to Tommy for their role in Bill's deception. "Cynthia, I tell you all the time, keep outta other people's business. What the hell you got to do with who's gonna get what outta what?" (*Wine,* 146). Though she has not been totally deluded by the male rhetoric of the black consciousness move-ment, she has certainly accepted female subservience and the proselytiz-ing of other women for the male cause.

The sociosexual hierarchy in which man is "mounter" and woman is "mounted" is not the acknowledged norm of the black society of *Wine in the Wilderness* but rather it is the ideal toward which Cynthia believes it should strive. Cynthia shares the view of Bill and Sonny-man that "the problem with the black subculture . . . is that it is a matriarchy in which woman is mounter, thereby depriving black men of their masculine role."[8] She counsels Tommy that her lack of attractiveness to Bill emanates from her excessive brashness, independence, and dominance. The only way Tommy can rectify her masculinized behavior is by returning the black man's manhood, by staying in the background and allowing him to pursue her. Cynthia enumerates ways that black women can empower black men to counter the debilitating "Matriarchal Society," but suggests no course for female empowerment.

According to Cynthia, Tommy's domineering nature has been formed in a matriarchal society, a society "in which the women rule . . . the women have the power . . . the women head the house" (*Wine,* 133). Tommy's refutation of the charge that she was reared in a matriarchal environment once her "papa picked hisself up and ran off with some finger-poppin' woman" makes profound sense and deflates Cynthia's fraudulent appraisal of her upbringing in a single sentence: "We didn't have nothin' to rule over, not a pot nor a window" (*Wine,* 134). Her statement succinctly dramatizes the fact that women who survive in the absence of men do not constitute a power structure and that their survival tactics are not emblematic of man hating. Furthermore, Tommy's blunt pronouncement regarding her and her mother's powerlessness exposes the myth of black matriarchy: that it means social, economic, political, and personal power, yet power in any form has been the primary feature of life to which black women have had little or no access. Iterating her powerlessness, Tommy refuses to assume any responsibility for the loss of black manhood. "I didn't take it from him, how I'm gonna give it back," she rhetorically questions Cynthia (*Wine,* 134).

Cynthia's wry parting utterance to Bill, that his portrait of "Wine in the Wilderness" is "exploitation," supports the inclusion of the earlier scene where the women converse in the absence of the men and points to the possibility of women's exchange functioning as a vehicle for consciousness raising, leading to in turn to sisterly honesty and solidarity. Gayle Austin draws the following conclusion from the construction of a "women only" scene in *Wine in the Wilderness:*

There is in this play, unlike so many by male authors, a scene between women, between Tommy and Cynthia, in which Cynthia realizes long before Bill does that the actual Tommy is not of the image they had preconstructed of her. Tommy raises Cynthia's consciousness by sharing her experiences, which strike a note of recognition in Cynthia. This scene points out that race and gender liberation are separate but related pursuits for black women. The scene is permeated by a sense of honesty possible between women when they are not looked at by men. Such a scene is almost nonexistent in plays that do not portray women as active subjects. There is a power in women getting together that is dangerous to male dominance.[9]

A truthful reconstructed image of Tommy, an outgrowth of the women's dialogue, raises Cynthia's consciousness and her caution. Hesitant to protest more aggressively the use of Tommy as the matriarchal messed-up chick and thereby be categorized as domineering herself, Cynthia stifles a desire to repudiate the slick glamorized image of black womanhood that bears no resemblance to her either.

Tommy's Anger   Counter to the ineffectual anger of the street riot, the liberating forces of anger and self-reliance empower Tommy not "to wait for anybody's by-your-leave to be a 'Wine in the Wilderness' woman" (*Wine,* 148). Tommy fights for herself because no one else will, and her strong sense of values and self steer her clear of "take low" politics based on class and privilege. "There's something inside-a me that says I ain' suppose to let nobody play me cheap. Don't care how much they know!" she avows to Bill (*Wine,* 146). Recognition of her own self-worth allows Tommy to discount the false ideology that blames the matriarchal black woman for a legion of cultural, familial, and social ills. Rejecting educated black culture's view of her, she contends that "the real thing is takin' place on the inside . . . that's where the action is. That's 'Wine in the Wilderness,' . . . a woman that's a real one and a good one. And yall just better believe I'm it" (*Wine,* 148). True liberation, Tommy discovers, is an internal phenomenon.

Not "cold but utter perfection," not "messed-up chick," not "bitch," not "*the* sister" but her own inscription of self sets Tommy up as "creator; she becomes the true artist etching the complexity of what it means to be a poor woman of color." Her outbursts of spirit and anger against the prescriptive roles that men attempt to impose on her resonate with the message that "women must begin to name themselves, to express their totality, to fill up the blank page with recognizable images of women" (Brown-Guillory 1990, 108).

Mojo: A Black Love Story

Mojo: A Black Love Story advances the dramatic treatment of black unity between the sexes, while examining many of the intraracial issues particular to *String* and *Wine in the Wilderness*. The black domestic drama addresses racial self-hatred, oppressive bourgeois values, the devastating emotional and psychic toll economic oppression exacts on black sexual intimacy, and the black male's enlistment of miscegenation to combat feelings of emasculation by the black female.

Set in Harlem in the fall of 1969, *Mojo* features Irene, a woman in her mid-1940s who pays an unexpected visit to her gambler exhusband, Teddy, as he prepares for an evening out with his white girlfriend, Berniece. Announcing that in a few days she has to have surgery for an unmentionable disease, presumably cancer, Irene begs Teddy not to go out for the evening because they have unfinished business to resolve. The two reminisce about the volatile relationship they had together and the circumstances that led up to their short marriage and divorce 18 years ago. Three weeks into the marriage that she had proposed, Irene mysteriously disappeared, sending Teddy only a postcard from Atlanta that read by way of explanation, "Hey there, Teddy. Life is too short for you to be tied down . . . or me either. Forget it. . . . Love . . . Reenie."[10] One year later Irene asked for a divorce, with which Teddy willingly complied. Irene confessed to him that the reason she asked him to marry her was to have a baby sanctioned by a legal union. At the time she rationalized not telling Teddy about her pregnancy and leaving him, since, as she states, "I didn't think it was too much any of your business . . . because you didn't seem to love me like I loved you" (*Mojo*, 14). Shortly after the birth of their daughter Teddi, Irene, emotionally unraveling under the pressure of taking care of a newborn alone and greatly fearing that the baby would end up being knocked about like themselves, gave her up for adoption. Irene now recognizes that she was wrong in withholding the knowledge of their daughter's existence from Teddy. "As hurtful as it is," she admits, "it's your business . . . ain't nobody got the right to keep your business from you . . . even if it's painful" (*Mojo*, 15). Without adding to her guilt, a shocked but understanding Teddy receives the news that he possibly has a daughter somewhere in the world.

Realizing that external forces have frustrated their relationship, the two converse about the economic conditions that blight black lives, making it difficult for black men and women to love each other unashamedly. Irene acknowledges that they themselves have not been totally innocent in adding to black pain and suffering. In donning the African robes that Irene has brought with her, Teddy is inspired to roll dice not for gambling but for fortune telling, the purpose for which they are used in Africa. After receiving a succession of affirmative answers to questions about their daughter by "rollin the bones" (*Mojo,* 20), Irene will not allow Teddy to consult the dice about her upcoming surgery, fearing that she will be pressing her luck. The uncertainty of the future has taught Irene two important lessons. The first is to seize the day: "Teddy, don't put off anything you want to do until later. Ain't no later. Later for later. It's all now" (*Mojo,* 18). The second is the importance of feeling a good clear blackness in her soul. She knows she "won't make it" through surgery if it is absent (*Mojo,* 21–22). In essence, her will, her power to live, is dependent on knowing who she is, being in touch with her ancestral ties. An absolute blackness will be like a mojo, a talisman that will ward off evil and be her salvation. The play ends on a highly positive note, with the two dancing to African music while Teddy pledges his unending love and support to Irene.

Conspicuous Consumption and Black Exploitation Teddy calls to mind aspects of the characters Bill Jameson from *Wine in the Wilderness* and L. V. Craig from *String.* Just as Bill's Harlem apartment is a statement about him—his superficial preoccupation with things African expressing a false allegiance to black empowerment—so is Teddy's a statement about him. His "overdone room," with "too much crystal, too many telephones and jacks, figurines, satiny, overstuffed furniture . . . [is] an ostentatious display of all the gadgetry that money can buy"; it bespeaks his allegiance to money and affluence (*Mojo,* 5). A dining-car waiter turned numbers-runner and gambler, Teddy relies on clustered symbols of affluence to situate himself as a bona-fide member of the black bourgeoisie.

Teddy's conspicuous consumption suggests L. V. Craig's flaunting of material and monetary possessions to gain communal respect and envy. Disdainful of African icons and the black nationalism of Garveyism, Teddy is concerned only with his own economic survival. His indifference to the black liberation movement echoes the dismissive comments Craig levels against the struggle for racial equality. The movement's crying, marching, praying, and singing "We Shall Overcome" are demeaning acts that blacks should not subject themselves to "just to eat at some dirty, greasy hamburger joint" (*Mojo,* 8). The passage of a civil rights law "Don't make me no damn difference!" Teddy smugly tells Irene, who approvingly receives the radio announcement of a civil rights victory. He further doubts her sanity for responding positively to the news: "A lotta crap, alla that prayin and crawlin all over the ground, kneelin whilst the police dogs be snappin at your ass. Singin while whitey throw tear gas. You lost your mind or somethin'? Carryin on bout 'civil rights'" (*Mojo*, 7).

Just as Tommy Marie and Old Joe expose blacks' exploitation of other blacks, Irene confronts Teddy with their manipulation of the system and exploitation of the black masses. Purchasing a stolen mink coat from a junky who "was shiverin and shakin from head to toe . . . needin a fix," Irene is remorseful that she used another black for material gain (*Mojo*, 8). The circumstances under which she obtained the coat have negated her enjoyment in wearing it. Dismayed that "Some-a the niggers over here still sellin each other out . . . and robbin and muggin and hittin on the head and ransackin," she signifies that Teddy's "racketeerin" has been "holdin down" his own people (*Mojo*, 19). Unwilling to take responsibility for his share in the oppression of blacks, Teddy argues that blacks' exploitation of blacks has persisted since the slave trade when Africans sold one another to whites. He justifies his actions by maintaining that those who seek him out to gamble do so of their own free will. He "don't go to anybody's damn house and say . . . yall just gotta play the numbers" (*Mojo*, 19). Except for the nod to patriotism implied in government-supervised vice, Teddy makes no other distinction between the gambling business he conducts and the lottery that the State of New York operates.

The Denigration of Love Behind Teddy and Irene's volatile marriage and subsequent divorce is a background of economic oppression that greatly afflicts the private lives of many black men and women. For blacks who must humiliatingly perform the foulest and filthiest work for little pay, economic survival can become the horrific. Haunted by memories of the grotesque work episodes of his youth, Teddy recounts the chilling experience of pulling garbage that contained rats so large they seemed to dare him: "Openin up that stinkin, rotten garbage shaft took more heart than having some damn 'mutiny on the bounty'. . . . Them rats congregatin, baby, all along the basement steam pipes. Talkin bout were-wolf and space saucer . . . sheeeet. Try pullin garbage" (*Mojo*, 17).

Similarly, Irene's recollections of her days as an "attendant in the ofay ladies lounge . . . washin' toilets, handin out toilet paper . . . Pinnin up torn dress hems, wipin up the floor behind sick drunks . . . laughing at their 'Jew' and 'darky' jokes, wipin away their tears," are tinged with anger and resentment (*Mojo*, 9). The ofays, or white women, who used the lounge sought either to ingratiate themselves with her by telling her mammy stories or to patronizingly dictate to her what her racial sensibilities should be. "Each one of em tellin me how much they loved the colored woman who raised em or cook the meals or whatever, tellin me how I must or must not feel about the race problem . . . and how I must not hate . . . The same jokes, the same advice from one damn rest room to another," Irene bitterly reminisces (*Mojo*, 9–10). On a par with dehumanizing work, running numbers for a living does not instill pride and self-esteem.

Illegitimate means of economic survival hamper black intimacy and affection. The denigration of love to keep from appearing vulnerable informs a fractured male-female exchange. Love becomes embarrassing when money bars access to a gratifying quality of life for oneself and one's dependents. It also becomes embarrassing when they, in turn, criticize their provider for performing menial or illegal jobs to support them. Irene relates her early introduction to the deleterious effects of poverty on black love, marriage, and family:

> When we were around each other . . . it was all fightin and pokin fun . . . mockin ourselves. I believe niggers think it's disgraceful to love one another . . . fightin like hell to cover up what's in the heart. My daddy once said to mama . . . "Sheeeeet . . . what's love, what's that? Better git yourself some money." Sayin them things right in fronta me. I'm tryin to eat the little bitta grits and bacon and make out that I don't hear what I'm hearin. She say . . . "Nigger, get the hell out." He slam the door and gone. She sit down and cry . . . then look at me and say . . . "Gal, you a mill-stone round my neck." Ain't like no Teevee story with us. . . . Love is hard to live round when a woman is washin out her last raggy pair-a drawers . . . and her man ain't got a quarter to put in her hand. When it's like that it's embarrassin to love each other. (*Mojo*, 15–16)

The private experiences of blacks struggling to make a living belie television hype and white domestic fiction that depict fairy-tale couples and functional families living the American dream "happily ever after."

Feeling Like a Man Compounding the themes of denigrated black love, subverted black manhood, and the black woman's alleged role in its subversion is Teddy's attraction to an interracial relationship. From his perspective, Irene's giving her honest opinion of his racketeering is signifying, meddling in his affairs with the intention of demonizing him and stirring up ill-feelings between the two of them. Vulnerable and defensive, Teddy uses his white girlfriend, Berniece, as a hedge against

Irene's fault finding: "Get offa my back, Reenie. . . . that's one thing about that simple Berniece . . . she makes you *feel* like a man. She's white but she makes you feel [like a man]. If you wasn't on your way to the hospital, I'd knock the hell out of you, for underminin me. Berniece knows how to make you feel pleasant" (*Mojo,* 19–20).

Ironically, Teddy's feeling of manhood comes at the expense of Berniece's womanhood. Teddy is insensitive to his demeaning treatment of and references to Berniece. As his white token, he can disrespect her, lie to her, put her indefinitely on hold. In his telephone conversations with her, he abuses her and leads her to believe that he cancels their date because of "some Philadelphia business" (*Mojo,* 13). True, Irene has just arrived from Philadelphia but Berniece does not interpret "business" as a visit from his exwife. Seeing Berniece as simpleminded assures Teddy that he can treat her in any manner he desires; though she might complain, she will not terminate their relationship.

Treating black manhood as an amorphous state over which women and white men have total creative and destructive power is a protective shield behind which Teddy hides. He makes no distinction between *feeling* like a man, a fluid other-determined state of being, and *being* a man, a static self-determined ontological state. The black man's wail of needing to feel like a man is not unfamiliar to Irene. Exasperated, she tells Teddy, "Feel like . . . feel like . . . I been hearing that all my days . . . sound like my poppa . . 'I wanta *feel like* a man.' You wanta *be* a man . . . forget that *feel like*" (*Mojo,* 20).

White Berniece figures as a placebo for Teddy's black manhood, stroking his ego needs without challenging his behavior toward her and others. She is not a panacea, however, only a temporary psychological quick fix, who for the present is reaping the spoils of a past struggle in which she did not participate. Irene has known Teddy for better and for worse. Berniece, on the other hand, has not experienced the worse with Teddy, which would test the true limits of their relationship and perhaps make it embarrassing for them to express love also. Because the two have been "busy poppin champagne by candlelight" and Berniece has not "had to rinse out her last pair of raggy drawers or pull garbage" (*Mojo,* 20), the manhood Berniece allegedly inspires has not been undermined or challenged by oppressive forces. Teddy's knowing the difference between feeling like a man and being a man, regardless of external conditions, is crucial to black stability in all its dimensions. Irene's emphasis on his being a man and being one on his own account accents her belief that true black manhood comes through self-affirmation, not through the validation of others, and certainly not through the dispensation of white women.

Their embrace of an African ancestral past equips Irene and Teddy with the power to break through fear and the disgracefulness of love to communicate their true feelings. Replacing a bourgeois suit and mink coat with African robes, listening to African music, and discussing the meaning of Africa heighten their perception of their African and American pasts and their vision of future possibilities. Irene and Teddy comprehend that tomorrow is not promised; the time to celebrate, to say "I love you," and to know oneself is now. Only the knowledge of themselves today will make any worthwhile existence tomorrow possible. The emergence of authentic black love, unity, support, and spirituality that allow the couple to live fully here and now determines the happy ending of *Mojo,* not the question of whether Irene will survive her life-threatening illness.

Racial Adjustment

Creating black drama for black people in the purest sense, Childress in *String, Wine in the Wilderness,* and *Mojo* unflinchingly charges that blacks can often be more damaging to black development, self-esteem, and dignity than whites. All black drama, as Gayle Austin notes, "puts whites in the unfamiliar position of making the 'adjustment' to seeing characters not of their own race on the stage." Conversely, a black audience, viewing Childress's *Wine in the Wilderness, String,* and *Mojo,* "may have had to make its own 'adjustment' to her message" (Austin 1990, 91).

That adjustment challenges blacks to take a look in the mirror and, seeing uncomplimentary true reflections of classism, sexism, and black self-hatred, make a change. Long-standing social and emotional wounds among blacks and between black men and women must begin the healing process. Childress's intraracial revolutionary dramas assert that true liberation starts from within, with true self-knowledge, self-appreciation, and self-celebration; and that true mutual trust, support, and respect between black men and women can occur only with the full liberation and equal rising of both.

Chapter Four

"It's Nation Time": The Adolescent Search for Selfhood and Acceptance

A Hero Ain't Nothin' but a Sandwich (1973), *Rainbow Jordan* (1981), and *Those Other People* (1989) contain moving depictions of alienated and lonely teenagers faced with finding security, acceptance, and selfhood in social environs hostile to their development as emotionally whole individuals. The young protagonists of these works, doubting their self-worth and lacking the positive reinforcement of their "somebodyness" by others, shield themselves from the disappointment, indifference, and neglect of peers, adults, and community. Constituting the third phase of her writing, Childress's adolescent fiction portrays young adults "who feel rejected and have to painfully learn how to deal with other people." Creating characters with whom they readily identify, she instructs young readers that it is possible to turn lives of pessimism into optimism, since "all human beings can be magnificent once they realize their full importance" (Betsko and Koenig, 65).

Foregrounding the importance that adults play in assisting teens' successful search for selfhood is a fundamental goal of Childress's junior fiction aesthetic. Her plots resonate with wake-up calls for adult intercession in the lives of adolescents from all walks of life at risk of annihilation from substance abuse, emotional and physical abuse, peer pressure, and parental abandonment. Adult characters in each of her novels must transcend the barriers of race, class, gender, or sexual orientation in order to join hands and "pull together and rise, work united."[1] In *A Hero Ain't Nothin' but a Sandwich,* Childress enlists the black national unification refrain "It's Nation Time"—the title poem of Amiri Baraka's 1970 volume of poetry—as a similar intraracial wake-up and call-to-arms.[2] The refrain's scope enlarges, tacitly, in *Rainbow Jordan* and *Those Other People* to encompass all people—friends, neighbors, relatives, educators, politicians, and other concerned adults—whose time for commitment to the young is now, since in the past too many of them have been "on the nod" (*Hero,* 107). A crucial feature of Childress's vision requires adults to assume the weighty responsibility of providing stability, protection, and love for children with whom they might not share a biological kinship but a human obligation and bond. A concerted adult and adolescent effort, Childress advances, is essential to the survival of teens assaulted on all sides with both the problems unique to their passage in time and the problems that are a timeless part of growing up.

The success of *A Hero Ain't Nothin' but a Sandwich, Rainbow Jordan,* and *Those Other People* dispelled deeply entrenched myths concerning the inherent nature of young adult literature that abounded in the 1960s and 1970s.[3] Childress dispelled the myth that books for young adults, to accommodate low reading skills and neophyte synthesizers of literary details, must be stylistically stark—adhere rigidly to a simple, linear chronology. In each of her young adult novels, she assembles a gallery of memorable characters who narrate each of their viewpoints in a first- and second-person stream-of-consciousness monologue style. Each character speaks directly to the reader, emphasizing the impact incidents and others have on him or her. Childress's use of a number of speakers to express a coherent whole also supports the confessional tone and ostensibly unbiased exposition of each character. "[I]t also enables the author to clearly show the discrepancy between what one character thinks he or she is doing and what is perceived by the others, without violating the integrity of any of them."[4] The film *Rashomon* by Japanese director Akira Kurosawa influenced her decision to present each chapter as a first-person account:

> I was very impressed by the film *Rashomon.* A woman was raped; she tells her story and the other characters tell their stories. Each one's version of the event is reenacted within the film. But all were *lying* except one, who was observing from a distance. And when he tells what happened, you understand why all the others lied. But I do an opposite thing. In my writing, all the stories differ, but I see that you can get ten *different* stories out of people *all telling the truth.* We don't all view things the same way, each perspective is different. Many-leveled narration is something I do well. It's true to theater. (Betsko and Koenig, 65)

In their own voices the 11 narrators of *A Hero Ain't Nothin' but a Sandwich,* the 3 narrators of *Rainbow Jordan,* and the 10 narrators of *Those Other People* "tell the truths of their lives. . . . the unconcealed truth[s]."[5] Brilliant, multidimensional delineations of human psychology also increase as a direct result of minimal description and the absence of third-person omniscient intrusion.

Childress resisted the literary mythology that books written for teens must avoid taboo topics and generally feature white middle-class protagonists. She is uncompromisingly honest in depicting the harsh realities that often accompany growing up as they indiscriminately affect white and black, male and female, and the economically privileged and deprived. Taboos against profanity, racial tension, drug abuse, homosexuality, sexual harassment, teen pregnancy, infidelity, divorce, and the AIDS epidemic as appropriate adolescent subject matter are disregarded.

A third myth that her young adult novels negate is that teenage fiction must be antiadult, especially antiparent, since teen readers, desiring to achieve independence, would prefer to read fiction that excludes grown-ups. Starting in her adolescent drama, *The African Garden,* Childress makes a poignant plea for the presence of caring adult involvement and affirmation of somebodyness in the life of a young person. In the denouement, when Maytag Diamond Ashley is the first adult to show genuine interest in 10-year-old Simon Brown, the youth begs Ashley to take the room his mother has for rent in their tiny apartment:

> Oh, please rent the room. Maytag Diamond Ashley, . . . I want you to live here. It's awful small but you can stay in the kitchen a lot . . . and the rent is only eight-fifty a week, eight if you don't cook. If I was grown and payin' the rent myself, I'd let you stay here for free. You the only grownup I ever met who just *talk* to me like I'm some other person. All grownups say . . . "How old are you? That's nice." What's so nice 'bout how old you are? You got nothin' to do with that at all. Then they say . . . "Study your lesson so you can be somebody." Everybody is somebody even if they just a wino. Then they say . . . "How is the school?" Ain't that a question? The school is fine . . . it just standing there bein', a school. But how is Simon Turbo Brown? Please take the room.[6]

A final myth that Childress subtly subverts is the belief that teenage books with powerful social messages must be didactic and preachy. Clearly, the conventional messages of her texts issue cautionary advice "to say no to drugs," "to not engage in teenage, premarital sex," and "to believe in and accept yourself even if others don't." Yet her detached presentations of these messages permit her readers to weigh independently the life-altering and sometimes deadly consequences of succumbing to peer and social pressures. Childress points her readers, like her characters, in a specific behavioral and self-affirming direction, but they must arrive at their own conclusions and choices.

A Hero Ain't Nothin' but a Sandwich

Childress's deepening awareness that the safe, circumspect themes prevalent in much young adult literature through the 1960s had become politically and socially outmoded helped her to overcome her apprehensions about grappling with contemporary issues profoundly affecting teens. Her effort to bring the escalating use of addictive drugs among urban youths to public attention, "Dope and Things Like That," one of the monologues in *Like One of the Family,* had appeared in the mid-1950s, well before experimentation with illicit drugs permeated every segment of society. A desire that her adolescent writings serve as effective teaching tools of real human experience and not shrink from the shocking or controversial engendered the storyline of *A Hero Ain't Nothin' but a Sandwich.*

False Bravado Benjie Johnson, the black protagonist of *A Hero Ain't Nothin' but a Sandwich* who progresses through experimentation with marijuana, skin-popping, and finally heroin mainlining, exhibits a toughness that belies his youthful vulnerability. In denial, the 13-year-old Harlemite does not believe he is hooked. He thinks he can give up using any time he wants to; he just does not want to. Benjie's short life has not left him innocent of the menace of urban reality. Fears of being physically and sexually assaulted are daily preoccupations. Childhood for him has been virtually nonexistent:

Now I am thirteen, but when I was a chile, it was hard to be a chile because my block is a tough block and my school is a tough school. I'm not trying to cop out on what I do or don't do cause man is man and chile is chile, but I ain't a chile no more. . . .

My block ain't no place to be a chile in peace. Somebody gonna cop you money and might knock you down cause you walkin with short bread and didn't even make it worth their while to stop and frisk you over. Ain't no letrit light bulb in my hallway for two three floors and we livin up next to the top floor. You best get over bein seven or eight, right soon, cause seven and eight is too big for relatives to be holdin your hand like when you was three, four, and five. No, Jack, you on your own and they got they thing to do. . . .

Walkin through dark, stinky hallways can be hard on anybody, man or chile, but a chile can get snatch in the dark and get his behind

parts messed up by some weirdo; I'm talkin bout them sexuals. Soon's
you get up to leven, twelve and so—they might cool it cause they scared
you know where to land a good up-punch, dig? I say alla this cause it's a
fact. I don't go for folks cryin and bein sorry over me, cause I'm a man
and if I can't take it, well, later!" (Hero, 9–10)

To adults, Benjie's proclamation of manhood at 13 seems nonsensical.
Yet the street's rites of passage into manhood are as legitimizing as the
Jewish bar mitzvah or other coming-of-age ceremonies that induct ado-
lescent boys into their adult communities.

To be one of the crowd, Benjie must yield to the machismo initiation
rites of the street: he must accept all dares, participate in the drug culture, resist parental and legal authority, reveal no emotional weakness,
and show no fear of death. Benjie exaggerates the hallucinogenic effects
of his first high on marijuana, while false bravery results in his first use of
heroin. Teasingly, Tiger and Kenny, two of his junk bag friends, call him
"titty-fro"—the equivalent of "little kid"—since he is the youngest
among their truancy group who has not mainlined (Hero, 68). To save
face and appear grown-up, Benjie bluffingly asks for a hit of heroin,
although he actually hopes they will turn down his request. Their unexpected consent leaves him with no "manly" choice but to take the injec-
tion. To downplay his body's terrifying response to the chemical
stimulant, Benjie cockily declares that the "shit ain't nothin" (Hero, 69).

It is ironic that this act of false bravado and penultimate step toward
his downward spiral puts him in touch, fleetingly, with his somebodyness. Liking "how they watchin me and payin their respeck, lookin at me
like they know somebody fine when they see him—not just sittin back
like I'm nobody," Benjie temporarily rises in stature and esteem (Hero,
69). The reversal of his insignificance as a little kid among his peers
abates his fear of the deadly potential of the drug coursing through his
veins. The fear of death is less intimidating than the fear of being
nobody.

From Benjie's impoverished perspective, being a child is inhibiting
and oppressive, equivalent to slavery, unless one is a child of privilege.
Television programs and motion pictures depicting perfectly manicured
neighborhoods and air conditioned homes flanked by swimming pools
and luxury cars foster his contempt for whites—"the society"—and his
own deprived existence. Nevertheless, moaning the blues over one's
poverty and crying "whitey" are pointless to him: "If somebody stomp
you down and cuttin your air off so you can't even breathe your breath,

you think they gonna let up just cause you cryin bout the stompin they puttin on you? Hell, No! Fuck the society! . . . Lass thing the society can do for me is to boo-hoo and come on with that sorry-for-you talk" (*Hero,* 10). Proud, poor, young, black, and vulnerable, "Benjie, as a potential junkie," posits Miguel A. Ortiz, "is the ultimate repository for all the evil that racism and capitalism can inflict upon human beings" (14–15). These oppressive contending forces, conjoined with the decline and failure of the family and society at large to create meaning in the lives of children growing up in urban jungles, portend bleak futures for Benjie and those like him who are caught in racialized poverty.

Believing in himself and others is impossible for the ghettoized Benjie. Bitter reflections on his father's desertion feed his feelings of unworthiness and nonpersonhood. The fear of identifying with anyone lest he later be disappointed or ridiculed is expressed in his cynical declaration to his "step-father" that "we livin in a time when a hero ain't nothin but a sandwich—so don't strain yourself tryin to prove nothin" (*Hero,* 76). Colloquially, a "hero" in many sections of America is a small loaf of bread filled with various ingredients, such as cold cuts, cheese, sausage, and peppers. With the exception of Benjie's history teacher, who also falls from grace, all of the black men he knows are menially employed or hustlers on the street. With no discernible heroes in view and a chasm looming between him and the central adults in his life, a sandwich is the only object to which Benjie can attribute "hero" status. Like Holden Caulfield in *The Catcher in the Rye,* he categorizes adults as phonies who only give the impression of concern. Most, if not all, view him as nobody. To be truly enmeshed in the central infrastructure of his household, school, and community, Benjie needs adults to accord him "somebody" status now, not reserve it for when he is grown.

No Family Heroes Heroizing a member of his family is a distant prospect for Benjie, who possesses a crushing sense of alienation and nonpersonhood in his multigenerational household. He maintains a consistent emotional detachment from the three key adults in his life because he also feels their withdrawal from him. His eccentric, old-time gospel grandmother, Mrs. Ransom Bell, despondent over the realities of aging and changing times, recedes from familial involvement. Rose, his mother, longs to tell him about the promises of life and love but inevitably finds herself criticizing him. With no official family status, Butler Craig, his common-law stepfather, cosupports the household on a maintenance worker's salary but has little say in the rearing of Benjie. On the one hand, Benjie gives Butler "credick for being the coolest one mosta the time" (*Hero*, 12), but on the other hand, indicts him for monopolizing his mother's time and alienating her affection.

Benjie blames Butler's entrance into their lives for the destruction of his happy childhood of six, seven, and eight. "Cool with each other" then, Benjie has warm memories of Rose helping him with his homework and the two of them taking Saturday night walks to the newsstand, candy store, and bakery. The aroma of Sunday-morning coffee permeating their apartment and his grandmother's preparation of bacon pancakes assured him of their happiness as a family. Then, unlike now, they "didden have to be talkin it out to see" (*Hero*, 41).

Resentful of the appropriation of his "place" with Rose, Benjie is unwilling to "credick" Butler with surrogate fatherhood. Low self-esteem and a partial Oedipal complex condition Benjie to seize random opportunities to demean Butler in front of Rose to deflate his "biggityness." Thoughts of surrendering to a father figure are laden with mistrust, since his "blood father cut out on Mama . . . cause he didn't dig me" (*Hero*, 70). The absence of his biological father confirms Benjie's unwavering feelings of unimportance and the suspicion that his very existence is accidental. Butler tries to fill Benjie's need for a father with his masculine presence, but the teenager is convinced that Butler and Rose prefer not to have him around. How can Butler accept him when his own father rejected him? And how can his mother truly love him if his physical features, a constant reminder of a marriage gone wrong and a man long gone, evoke her sadness?

Rose and Butler's last minute invitations to include him on their evenings out exacerbate his feelings of unwantedness and exclusion. "Hey, you wanta go to the show, too?" is invariably the way that they extend him an accommodating invitation to accompany them. "They always say 'too,' and when they say it, I'm thinkin that me as the one more would be one too many," Benjie sadly reflects, feeling like an afterthought or needless appendage (*Hero*, 69). Benjie perceives Rose's romantic alliance with Butler as a threat to his security, especially since he wants someone in his life that will be "crazy" about him exclusively (*Hero*, 76). Rose will never choose Butler over Benjie, but Butler's presence indicates to Benjie that his mother's allegiance to him is, at best, split.

Rose as Antiheroine The politics of race, class, and gender predetermine Rose's displacement as a heroine capable of guiding her son successfully through self-affirming rites of passage into manhood. A poor, black, urban, single mother working two low-paying jobs to support herself, her son, and her mother, Rose spends little quality time with Benjie and has minimal control over her household's daily fluctuations. The stresses of routinely coordinating smooth exchanges and mediating disputes between Butler, her mother, and Benjie wear on her emotionally, compromising her control over her family and life. Financially incapable of dissolving a failed first marriage, Rose is unable to meet her emotional and physical needs in a common-law living arrangement that further detracts from her strength as the family's leader.

Besides his perception of her betrayal with Butler, Benjie's antifemale attitudes deprive Rose of his total admiration and respect. The sexism taught in the street that affirms real men do not submit to women and Butler's reductive address of Rose and her mother facilitate Benjie's marginalization of woman's importance. Benjie classifies the women of his house as "nervous," and his mother as "signifyin" when she stridently warns him against drug involvement (*Hero,* 12). Since "they only women," neither his grandmother nor his mother deserved to be informed of his drug usage by his teacher—there was "[n]o need to go to no lady bout this" (*Hero,* 15).

Butler's habit of calling Rose and her mother not by their names but by their age and sex further diminishes their identity and authority before the impressionable Benjie. Butler sets the bad example of referring to Mrs. Ransom Bell as "old lady" while "fixin" his voice as if he is "talkin to a chile." In place of calling Rose by her name he genderizes her as "Woman" (*Hero,* 105, 120). Benjie immaturely thinks that a 33-year-old woman does not have needs and desires that must be met. "Look like a old woman," he thinks, "would be satisfy just to be cool and be somebody's mother" (*Hero,* 102). Although it is more likely that Benjie will heroize someone with whom he sexually identifies, the chance that he will look up to a woman is reduced since societal respect, particularly male respect, for her personhood is as tenuous as his own.

Friendship Splits

Peer intimacy, trust, respect, and reciprocity are essentials of friendships at any age. Benjie's closest friendship falters and fails with Jimmy-Lee Powell when his friend outstrips him academically and athletically, throwing off the delicate balance of these essentials. Initially inseparable, Jimmy-Lee and Benjie are boon companions. Hero-worshipping his friend, Benjie is crestfallen when he does not make the basketball team but is genuinely happy for Jimmy-Lee, who does. Although at this juncture the boys' alliance is still intact, the first insinuation of a possible fissure is evident. Jimmy-Lee's ego receives the stroking it requires for the maintenance of a healthy self-esteem, but Benjie's does not. Slightly older, Jimmy-Lee evinces a maturity that Benjie has not attained. A high achiever, he controls the friendship, whereas Benjie, idolizing him, is satisfied to follow along.

The boys' contrasting responses to the street's drug culture reveal their different levels of maturity. Jimmy-Lee supplies the two of them with the first joint of marijuana that initiates them into illicit drug usage. Benjie, along with another friend present, immaturely feigns euphoria: "Uuuuuuu-weee, um high, man. Groovin, this is it, man. . . . This it! Live or die, make me no difference," he exaggerates. Inversely, Jimmy-Lee, feeling "sorta so-what," waits for the "dumb kinda don't-give-a-damn" pot high to pass (*Hero,* 24). Thereafter, Benjie continues to get high and graduates to mainlining. Jimmy-Lee, on the other hand, discontinues smoking because he has "got somethin else for a dollar to do."

More important, he finds incomprehensible "all that talk bout bein a chicken, if you don't let somebody use your veins for a horse racin track" (*Hero,* 23, 24). A definitive split in their friendship occurs "when one is caught in a habit and the other not." Jimmy-Lee explains: "I've seen it time and time, needles divide guys, because the user rather be round another junkie. He through with you because he thinkin you lookin down on him. You through with him because you get scared of him, he smells like trouble when the monkey rides his back. Soon he's got to hustle hard for the monkey, and he hangs out with nobody but other hard hustlers" (*Hero,* 87).

Acting cool and powerful is Jimmy-Lee's method of staving off surrender to the drug scene. Yet despite his academic and athletic achievements, Saturday grocery store job, and choice to say no to drugs, he is emotionally detached from his peers and wants release from his dysfunctional family. Broken on the wheel of racism, his father is uncommunicative, emotionally distraught, and spiritually bankrupt. His mother provides for the family the best that she can, quietly rationalizing her husband's volatile mood swings. Unlike Benjie, who prays for a friend, somebody to be "crazy" about him (*Hero,* 76), Jimmy-Lee, seeks a divorce from his family, neighborhood, school, and old buddies. Searching for physical and emotional solace, he wishes "there was some place to go without bein in trouble," somewhere "they'd help anybody even if they didden snatch a pocketbook or shoot up" (*Hero,* 85, 86). Encoded in both of the boys' desires is the human craving for total and unconditional acceptance and sanctuary before their sense of desperation has been forced to the moment of crisis. Antithetical to Benjie's outward cry for help, Jimmy-Lee's silent suffering represents the same plea for adult intervention and understanding.

School The racism, the neglectful white faculty, and the black self-loathing endemic to Benjie's school prevent it from offering its all-black enrollment a refuge and a moral standard if not quality education. Searching for the cause of Benjie's truancy and turn to drugs, a white counselor supplies him with reasons that Benjie mimics back to him to mask his true ones. "I'm saying," Benjie confesses, "how nobody understand me, my school work ain't comin long so hot, not got the clothes I want for school, and like that" (*Hero,* 89). In reality, one of the formidable reasons he turns from school lies within the school and the ubiquitous, subliminal, condescending messages that he reads on the faces of his teachers:

> I hate school, even feel bad walkin to the school, forcin my feet to move where they don't wanta go. Schoolteachers can be some hard-eyed people, with talkin eyes; they mouth sayin one thing and them eyes be screamin another. Teach will say, "Be seated and open your book to page one nineteen and be prepared to read as I call your name." But them eyes be stonyin down on you, speakin the message: "Shits, sit your ass down, open the book, and make a fool outta your dumb self when I start calling on the ones who the poorest readers."
>
> Thass the message coming at you from whiteys. Then you got the special look that comes by shortwave from Black . . . they lookin sad like they could bust inta tears and they be sighin and shakin heads while they eyes saying, "My people, my people, yall some bad-luck, sad-ass niggas." (*Hero,* 90)

Excepting Nigeria Greene, the black history instructor who detects Benjie's drug usage and turns him over to the principal, the teachers at his school are uninterested individuals who supply no positive imaging or engaging curricula to meet the needs and interests of their students. Public acknowledgments of ethnicity and cultural diversity are relegated to an occasional school assembly, not to the classroom, where the ramifications of racial difference are felt daily. With no unified cultural or scholastic mission and no active intervention in the lives of children slipping through the academic cracks under enormous social and peer pressures, Benjie's school is an antiacademic wasteland. The growing problems of theft and drug use among the school's student body do not morally challenge its white administrators, who continue their practice of looking the other way.

Three years away from the haven of retirement, the white principal of the all-black school, aiming to leave with his sanity and his pension, is biding his time. Harlem experiences have taught him begrudging respect for "the fifth, sixth, and seventh generation poor" whose poverty "is as complicated as high finance" (*Hero,* 57), but he avoids the escalating drug problem in his school. He witnessed the clamor of protests and negative media attention received by the principal of another school when a student died from a drug overdose, he perishes the thought of a similar incident at his school. Not unlike the parents of the children who attend his school, he fears the drug dealers and the violent potential of the students. It is, therefore, paradoxical that he deems himself the bearer of a burden for which he abdicates responsibility. "Cohen [Benjie's white reading teacher] and Nigeria," he laments, "brought the boy to my office. Those two men who have never seen eye to eye on anything got together to bring one more straw to this poor camel's back" (*Hero,* 58).

A white middle-class suburbanite, the principal figuratively loots the black school district where he works. He makes "his daily bread," as Nigeria points out, "in a dirt-poor, so-called Black Community and spends his pay in West Park Gardens Drive, or wherever the hell else he buses out to when the bell rings at three" (*Hero,* 48). The principal's noncommittal stance on drugs, his racial and residential outsidership, and his paralyzing fear of the children he is commissioned to supervise negate any heroic impact he might have on students and teachers under his jurisdiction. Between the faculty's "don't give a damn" posture and the principal's "afraid to get involved" attitude, Benjie's determination to be "gone . . . with my diploma . . . or gone without it" is understandable (*Hero,* 91).

Oppositional in their racial ideologies, Bernard Cohen, a liberal but racist Jewish instructor, and Nigeria Greene, a fiery black nationalist who makes racial pride the main course of study in his classroom, portray two distinct warring political factions whose unification for the good of the students appears doubtful. Both teachers, highly effective in their disciplines, instruct their seventh-grade classes in subjects that enslaved African Americans were denied knowledge of. Cohen turns out accomplished readers, while Greene recovers "the withheld truth" of black and white American history (*Hero,* 44).

An atmosphere of distrust exists between the two, since they both feel that the other's raison d'être is to sabotage the race teachings that each imparts to his students. It perturbs Greene that Cohen attempts to brainwash black students into believing that "most whites are great except for a 'few' rotten apples." Greene charges that Cohen, like most white liberals, would "rather ruin . . . [his black students'] lives by makin them think they're imaginin the game bein run on them than to save them with truth" (*Hero,* 42–43). Retaliating, Cohen, hostile to Greene's black liberationism, accuses the black history teacher of working up the students' contempt for him before they come to his class. To assuage his white guilt and their identification of him with white oppression, he questions, "Was *I* ever a slave master? Did *I* bring slaves over here? Did *I* ever lynch a Black? Am *I* the one?" (*Hero,* 35).

Conversely, Cohen disapproves of Greene's Africentric teaching methods. He argues that it is unhealthy for black students to learn nothing but their own history, black supremacy, and black power, which, paradoxically, is the exclusive instruction that white children receive with regard to their race. Self-absorption in his own victimization—the resentment he receives from his students—eclipses Cohen's sympathetic acknowledgment of the racial contempt that every black American experiences from the day they are born.

White power, control, and dominance tie Cohen to a teaching job he essentially hates. He does not continue to work at the Harlem school to make a difference in the lives of the students. His commitment resides in resistance to losing his seniority by default to blacks. If he leaves it will be easier for those of the opposing race to take all the best jobs. He fears that if all black schools get all black teachers, blacks will move to the assistant principal and principal jobs "like Grant went through Richmond" (*Hero,* 35). Espousing Booker T. Washington's ideology that blacks restrict themselves to industrial trades, Cohen rejects black inclusion in the arts and educational professions. "In education, we," he states, meaning *whites,* "have absorbed more than our share of Blacks, we really have. A few more Nigeria Greenes, and we will succeed in cutting our own throats" (*Hero,* 36).

Paralleling the principal's avoidance of the growing drug problem, Cohen chooses to do nothing to intervene and reclaim Benjie as he nods under the influence of heroin in his classroom. He justifies his negligence, using his whiteness as a scapegoat. "Remember, I'm whitey. Nobody needs to hear me call Benjie or any other Black kid a junkie. . . . I'm not turning in anybody. The parents get upset, the principal gets upset, the kid feels betrayed," he contends (*Hero,* 37–38, 49). Preserving a low profile and the school's status quo are more important.

A penetrating black awareness guides Greene's comprehension that the latest race war is being fought within the confines of his people's very own veins and that the nation of blacks is losing the assault. He alerts his students that "It's Nation Time!"—time as a people to take the offensive against the powers committed to annihilating them as a race (*Hero,* 46). Fortunately for Benjie, Nigeria Greene acts on the convictions of his beliefs. Entering Cohen's classroom to examine a drug-nodding Benjie, Greene is unaffected by Cohen's fear of the "upsets" or the feeling of betrayal that exposure of Benjie's drug habit will arouse. "Right," Greene affirms, "but let all that happen rather than see the boy dead, let's don't kill him outta the kindness of our hearts" (*Hero,* 49).

Calling him "Africa," a cool nickname short of disrespectfully calling him by his first name, "Nigeria," the black students admire Greene's masculinity, independence, and assertiveness. He represents for many of them an abiding black pride not evidenced in any other segment of their lives. Benjie idolizes Greene; the betrayal Benjie feels when Greene turns him in for being stoned in school is therefore particularly crushing.

The Toughest Form of Street Temptation Childress considered removing Walter, "the pusher," from *A Hero Ain't Nothin' but a Sandwich* because "the villain was too persuasive, too good at self-defense, too winning in his sinning." She decided to "let him live" because "he is the toughest form of street temptation," and his deadly impact on any community cannot be minimized, ignored, or avoided. Divorcing herself from her own "conscious theories and beliefs," Childress allowed Walter to voice his own explanation of the misery he doles out on the street to adults and children alike ("Candle," 116).

Walter presents himself as a shrewd businessman who is simply participating in free enterprise. Meeting demand with supply, he is blameless of soliciting addicts or "pushing" drugs, since junkies seek him out. Feeling no contrition over his participation in creating young addicts, Walter rationalizes his choice to sell to them from the position that if he does not they will solicit junky middlemen who will "take a cut outta they [drug] bag for hisself" (*Hero,* 61). An absolute governing sense of business blunts his sympathy for his customers. Walter "[s]ometime . . . feel sorry for a guy who's carryin a monkey, but I don't feel sorry long. Feelin sorry ain't good business . . . Nothin is for free . . . not even a *feelin*" (*Hero,* 62, 64).

The hierarchical structure of his business requires that Walter first pay from his drug profits corrupt cops who, pimping off him, consent to look the other way while he conducts his street trade. For those under the naive illusion that the drug culture begins and ends in the black ghetto, Walter emphatically clarifies that white racketeers are the chief executive officers of the illegal drug industry: "If I was to get bumped or go to jail for life, these crackers who own the world and all what's in it would go right on doin like they been doin, just as if my ass had never been born. They haulin horse into the States by the ton . . . ain't most of it gettin here in nobody's suitcase, or sewed up in a dollbaby . . . that's some dumb-ass idea yall done picked up from TV" (*Hero,* 62).

Condemnation of blackness and black disunity engenders Walter's approbation of black annihilation. A nonuser—"if a fix could fix things" he would shoot skag himself (*Hero,* 64)—Walter hates himself for being born black and impotent in a white-dominated world. The weakness of "supersmart" junkies who are not dumb, just into a "dumb action" (*Hero,* 63) that the white power structure controls, typifies the racial weakness that he himself feels. He despises blacks' yielding of power to whites, viewing their weakness as grounds for his own exploitation of them. His disdain for the egoism of black parents who irresponsibly relegate the rearing of their children to others, and for blacks whose only instance of togetherness is the common grave that the state provides for them after they have overdosed, exonerates him. Euthanizing those blacks who "wanta die" by helping them "to slowly make it on outta here with a smile on their face" and a smile on his (*Hero,* 64–65) signifies the pusher's foremost conscious desire to exorcise blackness from his midst.

Butler's Transformation into Hero Benjie's drug crisis transforms Butler from a hard working black man enmeshed in his own personal pursuits into a committed surrogate father willing to go the distance for the preservation of young black manhood. A thwarted artist whose own addiction is the saxophone, Butler early in life chose personal survival over his art. Pride in his masculine self-assertiveness directed his choice; working as a blue collar laborer was preferable to being a starving artist, turning to drugs, stealing from others, or living off of a woman. He knows from personal experience the gritty moral challenges facing the black man and so is reluctant to judge Benjie's absent father. His own incomprehensions of self allow for the possibility that Benjie's father may not know or understand himself either.

By and large, Butler is a pragmatist where Benjie's addiction is concerned. He understands how Benjie became involved with drugs, but the more pressing question he must answer is how to get him out of the clutches of addiction. Rose's attempt to scare her son into recovery by taking him to the funeral of Kenny, the 15-year-old who, unbeknownst to her, gave Benjie his first fix, is ludicrous to Butler. "You can't scare nobody into bein well," he asserts. "If you could, jails and hospitals all be empty" (*Hero,* 118). Intuiting that Benjie's drug problem originates from psychological issues more complex than the red bicycle that he did not get for Christmas or the baseball game he never attended does not, however, preclude his own temporary avoidance of the problem. When detoxification and forgiveness do not rehabilitate Benjie, who then steals Butler's suit and overcoat to sell for a fix, Butler removes himself from the problem into the nearby apartment of Miss Emma Dudley. Hypothetically, poverty keeps Butler from acting on his wish to send Benjie on a therapeutic trip of an indeterminate length to a southern farm. Such a trip for Benjie, however, would figuratively be tantamount to a second paternal abandonment.

Butler and Benjie simultaneously undergo epiphanies of acceptance of each other at a moment when both are faced with life and death decisions. Foiling Benjie's attempt to steal a toaster from Miss Emma Dudley's apartment, Butler chases Benjie, who foolishly tries to jump from a 12-story rooftop to an adjacent roof and falters. Butler grabs Benjie by the arm in the nick of time and must decide whether he has the strength and the will to pull a dangling Benjie back to safety. Conversely, Benjie, who verbalizes death wishes throughout the novel, entreats Butler to let him plunge to his destruction.

Butler admits to running away from Benjie because he felt no true obligatory bond. Flight seemed an easier way of coping with the thieving-addicted Benjie, a roadblock to a peaceful relationship with Rose. "If this was my flesh-and-blood child," Butler confesses, "I wouldn't have run when he stole my suit . . . I went off cause he wasn't mine" (*Hero,* 110). Committed literally and figuratively to joining hands and pulling to save Benjie's life, Butler divines that as a black man and as a nation of one his acceptance of Benjie "can do what social worker, head shrink and blood kin can't—give a boy back to himself, so he can turn man" (*Hero,* 124).

The power of the individual to transcend any human obstacle is the first lesson that Butler imparts to Benjie to refute his insistence that someone must believe in him before he can kick his addiction. "Dammit, Benjie," Butler exclaims, "you gotta do it even if *nobody* believe in you, gotta be your own man, the supervisor of your veins, the night watch-man and day shift foreman in charge-a your own affairs" (*Hero,* 120).

Benjie's turning point comes when he is convinced that he can trust another human being to embrace him despite his flaws. Butler is not

Benjie's emotional crutch but his validation of worthiness and beacon of future stability. Benjie's perseverance in writing "BUTLER IS MY FATHER" 100 times during an episode of the nervous shakes of drug withdrawal exemplifies the stabilizing strength that the new father-son alliance has wrought.

Erasure of the myth propagated by educators, counselors, and the like that heroes, especially for black children, must be larger-than-life achievers is crucial for young people who think of themselves and the adults around them as insignificant and expendable. *A Hero Ain't Nothin' but a Sandwich* points to the ordinary individual who faces unswervingly the challenges of each new day as the real hero of the community. Butler Craig's working class credentials are the corrective for the larger-than-life mythic hero:

> Today the adviser told me Benjie needs "some male hero figure he can identify with," then goes to showin me a lista books bout Black History also tellin bout "colored" movie stars and great sports figures and how I must take Benjie to movies and ball games so he can see more heroes.
>
> I gave the adviser some advice. I say, "Some these big-time, celebrity-high-lifers can't take care-a themselves, they in as much trouble as you and Benjie. Yall gotta learn to identify with *me,* who gotta get up to face the world every damn mornin with a clear head and a heavy heart. Benjie once told me a hero ain't nothin but a sandwich—and you say a hero is a celebrity! Listen to *my* credentials; then maybe yall can pin me on a hero button. I'm supportin three adults, one chile, and the United States government on my salary . . . and can't claim any of em for tax exemptions. So, explain me no heroes. (*Hero,* 126)

The characterizations of Butler and Nigeria Greene reverse the portraits of emasculated and "no count" black men that appear all too frequently in the literature of black women. Moreover, they subvert the prevalent claim that black men are unwilling to support and participate in the nurturing and rearing of children. *A Hero Ain't Nothin' but a Sandwich* concludes with Butler, who has taken time off from his maintenance job, waiting outside the drug rehabilitation clinic for Benjie to arrive for his scheduled meeting. This is Benjie's second appointment; he missed the first. Undaunted, Butler is committed to Benjie for as long as it takes to get him there. Butler sends his newly adopted son affirmation of his faith in him as he waits: "I believe in you . . . Benjie, don't hold back, come on, I'm waiting for you . . . hurry up, I'm waitin, boy . . . I'm waitin right here . . . It's nation time . . . I'm waitin for you . . . (*Hero,* 127).

Rainbow Jordan

The dedication of *Rainbow Jordan,* "To those being raised by other than their natural parents—because I have shared your experience—and to all who care about us," links Childress to the title character of her second junior novel.[7] Reared from five years of age to her early teens under the watchful tutelage of her maternal grandmother, Eliza Campbell White, Childress knew the emotional and physical absence of her biological parents. She also knew the sheltering benefits of having a mature mentor to guide her through many of life's early pleasures and pains. Autobiographical strands, such as her grandmother's exposing her to art, culture, and the plights and progress of other women, connect the real-life Eliza and the fictional Josephine Lamont (Miss Josie), who becomes Rainbow Jordan's guardian, teacher, and surrogate mother.

The narration of *Rainbow Jordan* deviates from its male-centered predecessor, *A Hero Ain't Nothin' but a Sandwich.* In an alternating narrative structure, three female voices speaking across three generational lines construct the internal monologues of the text. Unlike *Hero,* however, "in which the several narrators were used to intensify the picture of the protagonist, [*Rainbow Jordan*] shows both the pattern of the generations and the individuality of each speaker."[8]

Fourteen-year-old Rainbow Jordan, the main protagonist and central speaker, is forced to be self-contained about her mother's three-time abandonment of her. Perceptive beyond her years, Rainbow knows that Katherine Jordan [Kathie] periodically leaves her to fend for herself, as she does at the opening of the novel, not because she has to but because it is her choice. As Rainbow's story commences, her caseworker Mayola must place her in interim care with Josephine Lamont until Kathie can be located or reappears. "What else is it but *abandon,*" Rainbow asks rhetorically, "when she walk out with a boyfriend, promise to come home soon, then don't show?" (*Rainbow,* 7).

Kathie's maternal rejection is felt early by Rainbow, who "never really had a mama and a daddy" but "got a Kathie and a Leroy" (*Rainbow,* 9). Daily, she walks a tightrope of hiding her mother's illegal and embarrassing negligence from Mayola, her girlfriend Beryl, her boyfriend Eljay, and Miss Josie. Growing up without adequate parental guidance, Rainbow knows more about loneliness and loss from a course that she takes at school entitled "Death Studies" than she does about adult companionship and the joys of family life.

Twenty-nine-year-old Katherine Jordan has little education and no formal skills, and she vacillates between being overly protective of and abusive to her daughter. Her job as a go-go dancer indicates that she is unwilling to relinquish a freewheeling past as a good-time girl. Stranded out of town on a dancing gig with her most recent boyfriend, Burke, she is in no hurry to return to the Harlem apartment where she has left Rainbow alone. Resentful of Rainbow, who is a constant reminder that time is passing her by, Kathie regrets the early sexual promiscuity that led to pregnancy and pushed her prematurely into marriage and adulthood. "One mistake I have to look at each and every day," Kathie laments, "is my daughter, Rainbow; the other I telephone now and then . . . my ex-husband, Leroy. Fifteen was too young for me to have a child. Mother nature made me able to give birth from the age of twelve . . . but she didn't bother to turn my mind on the same year" (*Rainbow,* 19).

Shrinking from motherhood, Kathie instructs Rainbow not to call her "Mother" but by her first name. A child having a child, Kathie sees Rainbow as a "playmate who came to visit but won't go home" (*Rainbow,* 135). During bouts of stress and depression over confining maternity, Kathie lashes out at Rainbow. Once when Rainbow drank the last bit of milk for which Kathie had other plans, she chased Rainbow through their apartment screaming, "I'm gon kill you! Wasn't for you I'd be somewhere. No man ever get serious . . . cause I got you! Damn stupid, greedy girl who don't know how to act!" (*Rainbow,* 11).

On those occasions when she leaves her daughter without adult supervision, Kathie blames Rainbow for not writing to Leroy for financial assistance. Guilt over defaulting on her maternal duty is absolved by plying Rainbow with gifts of clothing as peace offerings and material apologies. Her physical and emotional unavailability to Rainbow prevents Kathie from supplying stability or presenting herself as a positive role model. Her narrative voice, which is rarely heard, reflects her physical absence from her maturing daughter's life.

The voice of experience, 57-year-old Josephine Lamont, who passes for 50, is the stoic, interim care provider. She feels morally obligated to provide uplift and sanctuary to the socially beleaguered and arrogant Rainbow without admitting that she, too, is suffering from abandonment. In spite of her own shortcomings, Miss Josie's mature plainspokenness tempers Rainbow's youthful romanticism. For example, Rainbow's pride in her mother "lookin like a model" with long beautiful hair (*Rainbow,* 9) illustrates her youthful glamorization of Kathie.

According to Miss Josie, Katherine Jordan "looks like 'the lost girl' out of a TV show about crime and prostitution. A yard of wig hangs down her back to the hip. Her mouth forever shining with lipstick looking like a hemorrhage" (*Rainbow*, 15).

The individual biological cycles of Rainbow and the two women further highlight their generational differences. The commencement of Rainbow's menstrual cycle during an interim stay at Miss Josie's apartment marks her budding womanhood and sexuality. A virgin, Rainbow dodges sexual intimacy with Eljay because she is fearful of an unwanted pregnancy and her mother's wrath. Pressure from peers and the apprehension that other girls will satisfy her boyfriend's libido place her in limbo concerning her next move.

Kathie, at the peak of her physical beauty and sexual responsiveness, involves herself in a cycle of abusive sexual relationships with men to whom she knows she will never commit herself. Her current affair with Burke, a jealous alcoholic who slaps her around and threatens to take her life if she is ever unfaithful, evidences her participation in her own victimization. Intellectually, Kathie admits her unhealthy involvements with violent men, but sexual impulse and male dependency control her body.

Menopausal, Miss Josie is completing the biological cycle that Rainbow has just begun. With her sexual prime behind her, her husband Harold leaves her for a woman half his age. Without hope of salvaging the marriage, she weathers spousal rejection, injured self-worth, and financial instability, anticipating the strong likelihood that her senior years will be devoid of male companionship and intimacy.

The politics of reproduction and gender-biased sexuality complicate Rainbow's journey toward young womanhood. Nothing in her formative years has prepared her for physical intimacy. With sex nowhere in fairy tales—Cinderella and Sleeping Beauty fell in love and rode off into the sunset with their princes with no mention of sex—no blueprint on how to handle the issue with her boyfriend is readily at hand. Her mother, refusing her access to sex education in school, wants to keep her carnally ignorant. And the topic of sex makes her teachers and Miss Josie, who does consent to sex education, sad, upset, nervous, and evasive. Adult reassurances that sex is a natural function ring hollow. "If it's a natural thing," Rainbow speculates, "how come everybody acting weird about it?" (*Rainbow*, 117).

The double standard of sexual involvement elevates Rainbow's anxieties. Unmarried girls and young women who become pregnant are "bad," "disgraced," or "unwed mothers," while the boys and young men who impregnate them are viewed as "trapped" and never referred to as "unwed fathers" (*Rainbow*, 43). Rainbow's education regarding the socially inscribed inequities between the sexes introduces her to the gender-biased consensus that "boys will be boys," which fully exculpates male sexual behavior that goes against the moral grain.

Developing a balanced and healthy view of sex is difficult for Rainbow when sex is perpetually shrouded in mystery and yoked with violence and perversion. On the day she plans to surrender her virginity to Eljay, her fear of entering a park where a young girl was raped and murdered symbolizes her sexual angst and desire to avoid sexual consummation. Contributing to her association of sex with violence are the exploitative relationships that her mother conducts with physically abusive men. Her earlier viewing of a restricted movie conjures up other fearful and repulsive sexual associations:

> I saw a R picture where this girl, not lookin no older than me, turned her naked behind right up to the camera. Man sittin next to me was suckin in his breath, moanin and gaspin in a disgustin way. Beryl and I had to get up and move to another seat. He reminded me of a repairman who tried to take advantage and feel my bosom. I had asked him to please close a window in the school hall. If he had made a pass or *ask* me somethin . . . I coulda dealt with that and turn him off. He was sneaky, act like doin some awful thing. Sure wasn't thinkin nothin beautiful bout sex. He was ready to brute-out! (*Rainbow*, 117)

The lewd provocation of the unclothed girl in the film and the pedophilia of the repairman heighten, reluctantly, Rainbow's identification of herself as a sexual being and potential sexual object. When she was little, adults raved at how cute she was. Now, at fourteen, she gets on most people's nerves, "except for men," who look at her legs. Even Mr. Hal, Josie's husband, had looked at her legs during her previous stays with the Lamonts (*Rainbow*, 132).

Eljay psychologically punishes Rainbow for not giving in to the pressure to have sex with him. In trying to get her to conform to his sexual will, he tells her she might be a "dyke-lesbian" (*Rainbow*, 111), refuses to speak to her for a week, and calls her "too chicken to make a womanly move" (*Rainbow*, 113). Eljay foists onto Rainbow the responsibility of keeping in check his own raging hormones. The sexual tension he feels is her fault; thus he recommends that they "stop hangin out together" because she keeps his "nerves tore up" (*Rainbow*, 58).

Eljay's eagerness to engage in sex without weighing the life-altering consequences of his actions underscores his emotional unpreparedness for physical intercourse. One indicator that he is incapable of handling a sexual relationship is his resistance to using proper sexual terms because they are "square." A second indicator is his relegating to Rainbow full responsibility for contraception. His preference is to practice withdrawal because "rubbers" are "old-timey" and are only necessary to prevent disease. And as he tells Rainbow, "We not diseased" (*Rainbow,* 112). He feels no obligation to accompany her to a planned parenthood clinic or help with the cost of purchasing the birth control pills or other contraceptives for *her* to use. And, of course, abstinence is out of the question.

Most telling is his position that the female in a sexual relationship is solely responsible for the offspring issuing from it. Beryl, the pregnant girlfriend of his friend Buster, is a prime example: she's "regular enough to go on and have a baby without complainin" about Buster's failure to commit to her. "She facin the music like a stone woman," Eljay asserts (*Rainbow,* 111–12). Despite his pretense to the contrary, love does not enter into the sexual contract he tries to negotiate with Rainbow. Only after her prompting does he tell Rainbow that he loves her. Eljay's separation of these two powerful human forces demonstrates that the emotion of love and the biology of sex can be and often are unconnected.

Beryl, Rainbow's closest girlfriend since her best friend moved away, has been the principal female proponent of Rainbow's sexual initiation. Too sexually advanced for her years, Beryl gives Rainbow a book with 90 sexual positions complete with real-life illustrations. She subtly encourages Rainbow to make extra pocket money the same way she does— prostitute herself to Don, a pedophile, who pays three or four dollars for a quick look and feel. Beryl levels the most formidable peer pressure on Rainbow to join "the club" of girls who "turn on" for their boyfriends. She informs Rainbow that "Everybody who turns on is really laughin at how Eljay beggin you and gettin nowhere. . . . All I ask is where you comin from? Do you think you better than I am cause I turn on for Buster? You think you too good to give up for a fella you love? Feel like I'm friends with somebody who lookin down on me. . . . Other people saying you do . . . the 'in' girls" (*Rainbow,* 61–62).

The segregated sisterhood and misogyny among women that Childress assaults interracially in her early drama returns in her adolescent fiction as a deep-seated social malaise among young urban black women. Ridiculing others for being different and independent, Beryl and the "in girls" pimp for the males in their circle to assuage their own fractured egos and low self-esteem.

Miss Christopher, the gossip at Miss Josie's apartment who verbally assassinates the women residents, and Janine, whose freedom with sexual favors entices Eljay away from Rainbow, confirm Rainbow's observation that men are not the only underminers of women. Some women also relish sabotaging those of their sex:

> Miss Townes [a teacher] held a "consciousness raisin" session for girls . . . *feminists.* My conscious was raised fore I even walk in the door. All got to talkin how boys treat girls . . . but it stop right there. One thing I know, *females* can be extra mean and critical to each other. They need to break it on down and deal with that up front, before takin up males . . . and all that "awareness" shit. . . . Females be clawin the hell outta one another . . . hurtin each other bout their hair style, bout havin only one boyfriend or *none* boyfriend. Girls hate each other for bein too pretty or too homely, for bein too neat or too sloppy . . . or too loose or else uptight. But be callin each other "sister." Some in my school usin "sister" like just another word for *nigga.* They say . . . "the sister walked in lookin all wrong" . . . that's meanin your hair style or clothes or who you with or not with." (*Rainbow,* 89–90)

The young women of Rainbow's neighborhood falsely equate womanhood with the ability to attract and hold male interest with their sexually ripe and ornamented bodies. The sexually active Beryl and Janine, who wear skintight jeans, peek-a-boo blouses, and "boss" hairdos to attract the opposite sex are incriminating paradigms of misshapen female identities that rely on men to affirm their somebodyness. Building their popularity on the willingness "to make a womanly move," their antifemale influence engulfs other young women who desperately seek to be in the in-crowd. Fear of being unloved and left out "when the rest be paired off in couples" (*Rainbow,* 112) sensitizes Rainbow to the girl talk that snickers at her refusal to "put out" for Eljay. Wanting to prove that she too can make a "womanly move," she defies Miss Josie's rule that she not return to her mother's empty apartment without her in order to carry out plans for a midday sexual tryst with Eljay.

Miss Josie understands the vicious cycle of poverty and childbearing for which Rainbow is a prime candidate. Approaching 15, Rainbow stands to replicate her mother's life even in the type of first love she chooses. Josephine wonders "how long it would be before they [Rainbow

and Eljay] land in each other's arms and start the cycle over again . . .
children having children" (*Rainbow*, 18). To prolong that time, she recommends common sense and self-control without sounding preachy or
square. Speaking metaphorically of nature as a selfish bully who "shoves
and pushes" the young around, Josephine warns Rainbow not to let
mother nature decide her future too soon, since "she'll take over and run
you ragged" (*Rainbow*, 43–44). Sometimes it is best "to remain a girl
even when nature calls you 'woman,'" she advises (*Rainbow*, 43).

A balance of power and privilege, reciprocal honesty and trust, and
emotional availability is essential to a successful relationship between
Miss Josie and Rainbow. Miss Josie's evolution as a true friend and
"mother" to the maturing Rainbow is possible only when Miss Josie
reconsiders the wisdom of playing the role of the martyred woman who
must remain "the superior partner in the match."[9] Rainbow questions
why she must disclose her personal business about her mother and her
reasons for not having sex with Eljay as she had planned while Miss Josie
shares nothing about her private life. It is through the gossiping Miss
Christopher that Rainbow learns Josephine has lied about her age and
has not been forthcoming concerning Mr. Hal's extended absence in
Florida. Her discovery of hair dye, bleaching cream, and a see-through
nightie among Miss Josie's private things seemingly contradicts the
older woman's teachings on truth, race pride, and sexual virtue.

Before all channels of communication can be fully opened between
them, Josephine must acknowledge that because of pride she has lied
about her age and deceptively hidden the facts of her husband's abandonment, just as Rainbow has made excuses for Kathie's negligence.
Miss Josie confesses that she initially took Rainbow on as an interim
appointment partly for the money, but in time grew to care for her
deeply. Treating her less like a child and more like the young woman she
has become, Miss Josie gives Rainbow the letter from her husband
requesting a divorce to read aloud. The gesture of inclusion activates a
relationship of trust and sharing between the younger and older woman.
They have more in common than they had thought. Both know the pain
of male rejection after being displaced by another female, and both
know the treachery of navigating the transitions of growing older.

Mrs. Anderson, a socialite whom Josephine admires, and the black
movie stars and civil rights workers that Rainbow writes about for school
might be heroic models for many African Americans, but it is people like
Rainbow and Miss Josie, bonding in a restructured family, who are the
true backbone of black support and survival. Miss Josie's visit to

Rainbow's school as her surrogate mother and Rainbow's daughterly response to her signify that both have transcended the disintegration of their former family ties. Rainbow rebounds from a senseless attempt to give herself sexually, especially without birth control, to someone who cared little or nothing for her and accepts that Kathie will never return in full measure the love she gives her. Josephine ceases pining for an unfaithful husband, conceding that her marriage is over. "Gradually," Anne Tyler observes, "she and Rainbow come to care for each other— not in any instantaneous Hollywood style but with exactly the mixture of caution, hope, and suspicion that you would expect from two such battle-weary people."[10]

Those Other People

Jonathan Barnett's search for selfhood and sexual identity takes him on a circular journey of discovery. Escaping the conservatism of his New York hometown of Marsley Falls, Jonathan moves to Greenwich Village, seeking a Bohemian lifestyle in which individualism and self-expression are not censured. When Greenwich Village fails to provide him with the anonymity he requires, he takes a job in white suburban Minitown, where he must confront the most difficult admission of his life, his homosexuality. Coming out of the gay closet by declaring it to others seems ridiculous to him, since heterosexuals are never expected to announce their straightness, but before he can reintegrate himself in his hometown community and expect to be accepted, he must come to terms with self. Jonathan's initiation into adulthood and self-knowledge and the proclamation of his sexuality come after humiliating episodes of cowardice, thoughts of suicide, and intense soul searching. In his quest for selfhood, Jonathan learns that although there are some parts of himself that belong to him alone, there are also circumstances in which public truth and the good of the community supersede the individual's right to privacy.

Told in flashback, *Those Other People* commences on the night before the meeting of the Minitown school board at which Jonathan is to testify concerning an assault and attempted rape that he witnessed. The events of the last several months have profoundly unsettled his life. Much to his parents' dismay, he decides not to attend college after graduating from high school. After temporarily living with his aunt, he moves to Greenwich Village and secretly takes an apartment with Harper Mead, who is slightly older and also gay. The two become lovers but the relationship is brief. At Jonathan's first coming-out meeting, where he refuses to proclaim his gayness, Harper, bent on forcing him out of the closet, telephones Jonathan's parents and exposes his homosexuality. Jonathan returns home to confront the issue of his sexuality, but his parents, in denial, avoid the subject.

Wanting his own space, Jonathan takes a job as a temporary computer instructor at Minitown High School. Shortly thereafter he becomes embroiled in the racial problems facing the Tates, a black family integrating Minitown, and in a case involving Rex Hardy, the school's physical education teacher. A 15-year-old student, Theodora Lynn, has accused Hardy of attempted rape. Tyrone Tate, one of the two black students enrolled at Minitown High, and Jonathan are the only witnesses to the assault, which occurs in the school's basement closet. But rumor spreads that Jonathan is a "faggot" and the "nigger" is his "too-close guy," discrediting their account.[11] The only pieces of solid evidence that prove Theodora was lured into meeting Hardy, notes and computer disks, have mysteriously vanished from her desk. The notes and disks contain threats from an unidentified source that Theodora's previous molestation by her uncle will be made public knowledge if she does not comply with the directives given therein. To avoid scandal, Mrs. Mitchell, the principal, disregards her belief that Hardy is guilty and suggests that Jonathan be silent on his personal affairs and perjure himself by denying that he saw anything. Tyrone is willing to testify that Hardy assaulted Theodora, but only if summoned by a court of law.

On the day of the school board meeting, Jonathan chooses to announce his homosexuality and the facts of the assault to negate his own vulnerability to blackmail and to support the emotionally traumatized Theodora. While the school board and the Minitown community may find his sexuality morally abhorrent, they rightly perceive his honesty as heroic.

Being Gay Coping with the toll of being gay becomes increasingly uncomfortable for Jonathan. Joining any "big mouth" gay rights organization or "coming out" meeting to talk about gay courage and commitment where the goal is to say "My name is Jonathan Barnett and I'm gay" is odious to him. Gay men in the street who recognize his sexual kinship with them unnerve him, forcing him to turn away from their unspoken messages. Some look away first or sarcastically smile, "Hey Queen, who do you think you're kidding? I know you. Welcome to the club" (*People,* 76). The desire to please himself and his parents, and his pride in seeing himself as more than a social misfit or sexual oddity, fortify his resistance to his homosexuality. But running away from his sexuality is ineffective; "dropping out" from an issue so fundamental to his identity and so politically charged is not an option (*People,* 142).

Jonathan's narrative of Jim, with whom he has his first homosexual experience on Turnabout Mountain, illustrates that same-sex sexual curiosity is normal for most boys, and that many eventually outgrow or shun it. For others it is a turning point. Caught in an electrical storm that leaves one of their two sleeping bags drenched, the boys share the remaining dry sleeping bag and engage in fondling and intimate touching. The encounter is a passing phase for Jim but a revelation for Jonathan, a true turnabout for him, as the mountain's name signifies. Because of the taboo nature of the revelation, it cannot be dealt with openly. Jonathan narrates: "In the morning, we talked too loud, too much and too long about nothing in particular. After that night I was close to Jim, even though he sat on the far side of our classroom and lived on the other side of town. He was the first person I loved. We never discussed the relationship" (*People,* 75). Jim's mention of a "smashing" girl in a letter from England where he and his remarried mother move extinguishes the boys' correspondence and any further emotional investment on Jonathan's part. The encounter on Turnabout Mountain does not make Jonathan gay; it simply solidifies a pervading consciousness that he has been distantly aware of for some time but had neither the opportunity nor the daring to act on until then.

Jonathan and Harper Mead's turbulent relationship bears much in common with erratic heterosexual relationships, save on one score. Homosexuality, the common facet of their lives that unites them, that makes them accessible to each other, is also the very thing that gnaws at the core of their mutual caring and sharing. Six weeks after Jonathan answers Harper's room-for-rent ad, they convert Jonathan's bedroom into a film studio and Jonathan moves into Harper's room. The relationship deteriorates from the best into the worst Jonathan has experienced.

Pleasant evenings spent at the museum and eating out are offset by the "down side"—when Harper attempts to exercise dominion over Jonathan's life and shame him into admitting his homosexuality. It is true, Jonathan concedes, that he is not living with his aunt as his parents and friends think, and that the deception is to conceal his relationship with Harper. It is not, however, Harper's place or right to force Jonathan out of the closet before he is ready by telephoning his parents or later telling Rex Hardy that he and Jonathan were once lovers. Jonathan and Harper are equally cruel in their transgressions against each other, since one denies and the other forces the relationship. Both are also equally responsible for the termination of what is undoubtedly an uncommitted relationship.

Parental Denial Jonathan leaves Marsley Falls more for his parents' sake than for his own, since they are unprepared to meet head-on the awkwardness, embarrassment, and pain of acknowledging his homosexuality. Their self-professed liberalism—they support women's, gay, and lesbian rights and oppose racism—leads them to believe that they are not intolerant or bigoted people. But they soon discover that intellectualizing homosexuality is easier when the gay individual is not a family member. Hollow consolatory statements, such as "At least life goes on" and "Differences make the world," which Lila Barnett spouted three years earlier to a friend reeling from the revelation of her nephew's homosexuality, do not comfort now that her son's difference is in question.

Childress's portrayal of Jonathan's parents' suppression of his gayness illustrates that the fear of family rejection and ostracism can be the most psychologically inhibiting obstacle to a homosexual teenager's achieving self-knowledge and self-acceptance. Lila Barnett maintains that she and her husband never noticed any indicators of Jonathan's sexual difference. They have, however, resisted "tendencies" that subtly alluded to their son's sexuality as early as his eighth year. Curbing her son's "feminine" interests, Lila Barnett discouraged Jonathan from stroking lace pleasurably against his face and neatly arranging her nail polish and perfume on her dresser. Jonathan's father, not a man given to rugged activity, scheduled "roughing it" excursions to develop his son's masculinity. Conversations with his parents in his early teen years touching on his homosexuality met with a sudden change of subject or avoidance of the topic altogether. Both of his parents apprehensively waited for what they hoped would be a "passing phase" to run its course (*People,* 90).

After denial, the notion that Jonathan's obvious sexual confusion can be purged with the right dosage of heterosexual stimulation possesses the Barnetts. Seizing every possible opportunity to parade Fern, Jonathan's high-school girlfriend, before him, his parents selfishly use her, hoping to cure their son. Fortunately, Fern, a sensitive and perceptive girl, has been aware of Jonathan's sexual conflict and has extended him space to determine his leaning. Jonathan informs his parents that "Fern doesn't care to be my beard anymore"—a public mask to pass himself off as straight (*People,* 146). Heedlessly, Lila Barnett implies that Fern's love will somehow convert her son, save him from himself.

Jonathan calls his mother on her egocentric thinking: "If I had a sister—well, I mean if you and Dad had a daughter would you want her to marry a gay guy in order to try and straighten him out. The answer is no. No is the right answer" (*People,* 146).

A Homophobic Community Communal harassment exponentially aggravates Jonathan's sociopsychological displacement. As long as he is thought to be heterosexual, Minitown welcomes him with open arms. Mrs. Trale, his landlady, is maternal and warm, and the parents of his students are glad to have a computer whiz, even if he is only 17, instructing their children in the latest technology. As a homosexual, he is a perceived threat to the safety and well-being of those same students. Anonymous calls made to him by townspeople threatening him not to get involved in the Rex Hardy–Theodora Lynn case concentrate on his homosexuality, not the foulness of the alleged assault. Subtly pressuring him to move, Mrs. Trale demands that he pay his rent in advance and insinuates that the stray cat he feeds may have contracted the AIDS virus from him. Jonathan has done nothing unethical to compromise his professionalism as a teacher, yet rumors and innuendo turn him into a pariah. It is ironical that Rex Hardy violates the community's trust, but the Minitown citizenry, in spite of his offense with one of its female youths, continues to support him.

Lacking a supportive family, lover, community, and place of employment stresses Jonathan almost to the mental breaking point. He entertains recurring thoughts of suicide as the ultimate escape from his woes. "Taking my life," he thinks, "is a lousy serious idea. Especially since I haven't lived long enough to make an exit." Yet the lack of "someone to just listen" without ridiculing him is, at moments, threatening to his continued existence (*People,* 46). With or without a sympathetic ear, however, he resists suicide as an approach to problem solving. Mustering courage one day at a time to meet the social and moral challenges that besiege him is the only true way to transcend adversity, public and private:

> A full turn of this gas fireplace and I would not have to worry about anything anymore. Not Mrs. Trale, my father or mother, other people named anonymous, public opinion, Theodora Lynn's problems or Harper Mead. I'd be out, free. Maybe courage in general is what I lack. Now that's the gift for the boy who has everything, more courage. It takes nerve to exit, but now I know it takes even more nerve to live and face the daily music. (*People,* 76)

Facing the Minitown school board and declaring his homosexuality, not committing suicide, is Jonathan's ultimate act of escaping back to himself.

Female Sexual Victimization A thematic carryover from *Rainbow Jordan,* antifemale sexual politics constructs the heterosexism and cross-gender bias that Childress treats in *Those Other People,* as she examines the belief that the female body is open, vulnerable territory for male sexual objectification, victimization, blame, and abuse. To be popular, the girls at Minitown High condone a sexually exploitative initiation ritual in which boys trap girls in an empty closet or classroom for a fast kiss and a quick feel of their breasts and genital areas. Although these young women are experimenting with their sexual awakenings, their participation in sex games in which they pretend not to surrender their will validates the deeply ingrained male belief that all females unconsciously want to be raped. Often in actual cases of sexual assault, the male's projection of his own unchecked sexual urges and desires onto the female frees him from guilt of sexual misconduct by assigning her responsibility for her own victimization.

The sexually abused Theodora Lynn loses her innocence and develops an intolerance for and distrust of men. Coerced at the age of nine into becoming the "secret love" of her Uncle Ed, who lived with her family, the emotionally traumatized Theodora must now take clandestine trips out of town to visit a therapist. Six years have passed, but the recollection of the sexual acts her uncle pressured her into performing still makes her vomit. Cynical of most men, she states, "I didn't have to wait till I was fifteen to discover what a man wants" (*People,* 51). Thus Rex Hardy's attempted rape of her does not catch her naively off guard. Dubbed "Sexy Rexy" and "the mastercraftsman of the accidental bump" (*People,* 52), Hardy on numerous occasions has taken her aside under the pretense of an academic conference to make passes at her. Prior to the day Spencer Reese, a bigoted classmate of Theodora's, locks the two of them in the school closet, knee pats and a fast feel have been the limit of Hardy's sexual aggressiveness toward her. On the latter count, Theodora submits to Hardy's groping of her body because he has the power to report her for cheating on a math test.

At 39, Hardy projects his own sexual myths, repressions, expectations, and frustrations onto Theodora. He plays the same kiss-and-feel sex games as the teenage boys. He also blames her for her own victimization. "You keep it going, Theodora. You ask for it! . . . You're the one who keeps it going, Theodora, You ask for it," Hardy chants as he rips her tee shirt during the course of the closet assault (*People,* 117). Hardy's abdication of responsibility for his own sexual aggression mirrors the juvenile mentality of Spencer Reese: "Theo—I call her 'Hots'—is loose as a goose on castor oil. She sure knows how to show it all off. She's got a thousand ways of asking for rape. At school Theo throws one leg over her desk, playing cool while making guys sweat. She wears tight pants, or skirts so short you can see eternity. Just as I'm getting off on the view she pulls herself together and sits like a saint" (*People,* 132).

Hardy, like the young Reese, is contemptuous of women who are powerful and in control. The antiwoman joke he tells in a teachers' meeting approving the ancient custom of Chinese women walking two steps behind their men reveals his hostility toward women and his resentment of working under the authority of Mrs. Mitchell. His attack of Theodora is yet another outward display of his antiwoman hostility. An earlier assault charge by an underage female student at another school implies that he is developing a pattern of violence and forced domination over young vulnerable women. The closet in which he attempts to rape Theodora functions as a metaphor for coercive illicit heterosexual activity that needs public "outing" and intensive sociopsychological scrutiny.

The most unsettling projection of sexual responsibility and guilt onto Theodora for her own victimization comes from her father, Sam Lynn. Lynn does not hold his brother, an adult, totally responsible for the violation of his daughter. He feels that Theodora, even at the vulnerable, innocent age of nine, understood the gravity of her actions and willingly participated. "And don't blame it all on him. . . . Why the hell were you always in his room?" her father demands (*People,* 58–59). Lynn no longer speaks to his brother, not because of outrage over what was done to his daughter but because of a sense of awkwardness and a fear of confronting the truth.

Lynn avoided public scandal by sending his brother away, but the Hardy incident cannot be finessed as easily. Lynn's private shame that his daughter is damaged marriageable goods from the first incident and the suspicion that Theodora prompted the second attack magnify his desire to suppress any action against Hardy. Appearing to refuse to let her make a public spectacle of herself but in fact attempting to protect himself from public scrutiny, Lynn tells Theodora of her attempted rape that "the courts are not interested in what *almost* happens to people" (*People,* 60). To foil what he perceives as the right conditions for a third assault, he invokes myths about rape and black male sexuality by warning

Theodora not to sunbathe in her bikini in the backyard, in full view of their new black male neighbors, as if "asking to be raped" (*People*, 58)

Theodora's father intensifies the emotional trauma she experiences since his indictments of her on each occasion are the equivalent of another assault. If her own father, the central male figure in her life, does not believe and defend her, why should the community at large? Inattentive to her emotional and psychological needs, Lynn preoccupies himself with the value of his real estate now that the Tates live next door. "Are a house and new neighbors more important than a person who is your child?" Theodora demands of her father (*People*, 56). Tired of being taken advantage of and believing that she must fight the world alone, Theodora charges Rex Hardy, despite her parents' push to dismiss the whole affair.

Racial Intolerance The supporting theme of racial bigotry complements the novel's treatment of sexual abuse. Childress indicts passive and covert racism as one of the most damaging legacies parents pass on to their children. Through the eyes of Theodora, her father is not a racist like many of his friends, but the same racism that does in fact exist in him also exists in her. Sam Lynn regards the Ku Klux Klan as too subversive but believes wholeheartedly in racial segregation. Blacks should stay in their neighborhoods, where crack cocaine and murder are rampant. When he purchased his house he signed a restrictive clause to ensure that nonwhites were kept from moving into the neighborhood and downgrading property values. Blacks who are comedians, sports figures, and singers comprise his limited list of acceptable blacks. But even those blacks would not be welcome next door. His racist beliefs persist, even though the Tates are progressive, business oriented, and affluent. Mrs. Lynn supports her husband's bigotry. She tells Theodora that white girls should not be paired as work partners with black boys in the classroom and that Jonathan Barnett has unwisely teamed her with Tyrone Tate in computer class. Alluding to blacks, she instructs her daughter not to associate with the wrong kind of friends. Theodora must leave for school after the Tates' departure to ensure that she does not encounter them along the way.

On friendly terms with the Tates, Theodora still has skewed ideas concerning racial difference. Her conception of what constitutes "acceptable" behavior on the part of blacks is, like her father's quite narrow. Hank Thompson, a black tap dance instructor who left Minitown unexpectedly at the end of the last school term, is her prototype for the acceptable black—a cross between the happy-go-lucky minstrel figure and the devoted servant. She "never once saw him when he wasn't smil-

ing," and "[h]e would do you a favor in a minute without your even asking." Theodora subverts Hank's blackness, his outward racial difference,
instead of acknowledging it as an essential part of who he is. "Oh,
nobody cared or even noticed how dark he was," she offers, to substantiate his acceptability to whites (*People,* 54).

Spencer Reese's prejudicial instructions from his elders have trans-
formed him into a confirmed white supremacist. Spencer, whose father
encourages him to be the founder of the National Association for the
Advancement of White Power, outwardly proclaims his intolerance of
blacks. When Jonathan Barnett assigns him Tyrone Tate as a computer
partner, he immediately rejects the assignment on the grounds that he,
a superior white, should not have to work with an inferior black. Also
invoking the black sexual myth, he alleges that Tyrone has "one eye out
for getting a white girl" since "they [black men] all do" (*People,* 135).
Spencer equates being a "white" man with being a "racist" white man.
Observing that his father, Sam Lynn, and their buddies are losing the
nerve to take action against the black invasion of their community,
Spencer teams up with a friend of a similar racist mindset to burn a cross
on the lawn of the unwanted Tates. The two boys nearly burn down the
house of the black family, but Spencer's father congratulates the
unknown hero, stating, "Somebody in this town has guts. And whoever
he is, he made my day" (*People,* 137).

Fitting into the mainstream has meant erasure of self and black identity for the Tates. Since moving from Brooklyn's black Crown Heights
neighborhood, "lifestyle, "image," and "cross-over" have been the buzz-
words of the Tates (*People,* 168). On the other hand, "black" is a stigma-
tized word that they spell out and whisper like a terminal disease. Any
cultural marker announcing their difference must be eradicated.
Maxwell Tate, the father, bans the family from playing the music of
Ruth Brown, Billy Eckstein, Count Basie, and Billie Holiday, fearing
that whites might overhear and think they are common and indulge in
low-life habits.

The middle-class Maxwell Tate is an integrationist who dissociates
himself from the black masses. In conversations with his brother
Kwame, a black nationalist, Maxwell refers to blacks who embarrass him
as his brother's people and not his own. His income of more than
$70,000 a year from a hair-care products business, his residence in a
white neighborhood, and his recent acceptance into the white country
club constitute conclusive proof that he has made it in white society.
White acculturation and brainwashing are the side effects of the family's

cross-over lifestyle, and the strain of their integrationist accomplishments is more visible on Maxwell's wife, Arlene, and daughter, Susan. To fit the role of the upwardly mobile woman, Arlene diets herself from a size 13 down to a size 7. While performing mundane household chores, she constantly mumbles, "This thing has to work," referring to their uncertain residency in white suburbia (*People,* 37).

Of the two Tate children, Susan, on the threshold of young womanhood, feels more acutely than Tyrone the psychic displacement of living in a white community intolerant of their presence. At the stage of development where dating is important to her maturation, she has no potential male companions. Her father tells her that race does not matter, but her own observations speak to the contrary. She notices the "picky kind of racism buried deep down" inside Jonathan Barnett, who minimizes blacks' unique introduction to America via slavery by juxtaposing it with the immigrant experience (*People,* 67). She feels the hatred based on race passed between her father and Sam Lynn.

Racial hostility also permeates her own consciousness. It is Susan who took the notes and disks that would substantiate Theodora's claim of having been coerced into meeting Hardy, but she is unwilling to give them up. Why should she concern herself with the predicaments of whites? The self-interest of protecting Tyrone from involvement as a witness in the case comes first. Her father and Uncle Kwame ultimately decide to turn over the evidence to Jonathan, placing the fate of the notes, disks, and Theodora's case in white hands and absolving themselves of moral responsibility. The two men want "all concerned to know that the Tate family doesn't want any part of white folk business" (*People,* 171).

Silencing the Truth Suppressing the truth when dealing with controversy is the predominant adult model of behavior that Jonathan and his teen peers must surmount. "It goes right through me these days to see so many good folks scared to speak up against wrong," Kwame Tate ironically declares while he and his brother try to dissuade Tyrone from testifying to what he has seen (*People,* 170). Theodora's nonsupportive parents succeed in forcing her to drop all charges against Hardy, sacrificing the truth of her violation. Mrs. Mitchell's bid to sway Jonathan's testimony before the school board fails, but truth is still sacrificed to expediency and the school's untarnished image. Neither Theodora, who withdraws all charges, nor Hardy will return to Minitown High, and Jonathan, tendering his resignation, is no longer a Minitown High concern or threat. The board does not reject his resignation.

Speaking the truth and affirming his identity renew Jonathan's outlook on life. There are some parts of himself that belong to him alone, but there are some parts that belong to others. Self-knowledge, he discovers, is a precious truth that the truly mature individual reinvests in others. "Maybe," Jonathan speculates, there is "an income tax on knowledge, we owe some of it back" (*People,* 185).

Thresholds of Hopeful Possibility

Childress offers no easy solutions, no contrived happy endings, and no quick fixes to the identity crises confronting her teen protagonists. Her narratives of adolescence end indeterminately on the threshold of hopeful possibility. *Those Other People* concludes with Jonathan Barnett, now secure in himself, heading homeward to a dialogue with confused parents who still think that his sexual reformation is possible. The final implication, however, is that in time they will come to accept his homosexuality, even if they do not approve of it. With many differences still to resolve, Rainbow Jordan and Josephine Lamont move one step closer to a relationship of trust and openness. And in *A Hero Ain't Nothin' but a Sandwich,* Butler Craig commits to helping Benjie kick his heroin addiction for as long as it takes. To Childress's adolescent readers, these uncertain endings transmit no false security and no life-as-a-fairy-tale interpretations. Each story accepts the reality that the road toward selfhood, adulthood, and acceptance by others is rocky with rejections, disappointments, and failures. But with the personal stamina and adult support, it can be safely traveled.

Chapter Five
A Short Walk

A Short Walk (1979), Childress's second novel and first adult treatment, begins with the birth and adoption of Cora James in Charleston,
South Carolina, in 1900 and ends with her collapse and sudden death
on the streets of Harlem at the conclusion of World War II. The
account of Cora's "short walk from the cradle to the grave" touches on
the first wave of activism leading to the civil rights movement. It is
also, as Melissa Walker points out, "Dickensian in its sweep across the
social spectrum and its scanning of the effects of social policies on the
lives of individuals struggling to meet their needs in a society struc-
tured to exploit them."[1] The framing years of Cora's life represent an
important pivotal period in African American history. Joseph McLellan
explains:

> Cora James represents a transitional generation in black American soci-
> ety—the descendants of slaves who had to work out a secure new identi-
> ty in the first half of the present century. Victims of scorn or
> condescension by most of white society in their lifetimes, they have not
> always fared much better at the hands of the proud militants who are
> their children, but they did something that was both difficult and neces-
> sary, and on the whole (despite many failures) they did it well. In Cora's
> story, Alice Childress introduces some of the people who did this neces-
> sary work—people ranging from the black nationalist followers of
> Marcus Garvey to entertainers who had to put blackface makeup on their
> black skins to perform in minstrel shows. It is a story that should be
> known and she tells it well.[2]

The opening pages of the novel portend the birth of a new day at the
turn of the century for the next generation of African Americans. Mr.
July, a former slave who comes to pay his last respects to 16-year-old
Murdell Johnson, who dies within a few days of giving birth to Cora,
prophesies that the newborn's life will be racially unencumbered: "Most
forty years done pass since the last day a bondage, so Murdell's baby
gonna someday walk where we now can't go, live to say what we can't,
gonna taste the sweet years to come. Her life will live easy."[3]

Far from easy, Cora's short walk through life on both sides of the Mason and Dixon line is fraught with racist control. Yet compared with Mr. July, who would "ruther pick up behind dawgs than work for white folk" (*Walk,* 17), Cora "does go where he could never go and speaks what he could never say" (Walker, 92). Still, the racial progress that Cora and her contemporaries make in almost half a century seems trivial to the succeeding generation of blacks. Cora's daughter, Delta Garvie Anderson [Green], coming of age in the 1940s, accuses her mother's generation of complacency. Young and spirited, Delta will in time learn, like her grandmother and mother before her, that social protest results in compromise and failure as well as in advances for the cause.

Published at the close of the 1970s, when the futures of the civil rights and women's movements were at dubious crossroads, *A Short Walk* introduces a believable, impulsive, complex black woman of the not too distant past who is much in sync with contemporary feminism. Cora is unwilling to follow the counsel of her adoptive mother, Etta, that women must "learn to wait" and to "bide" their time against racist and sexist oppression (*Walk,* 72–73). Yet daily life instructs her that personal and economic survival for a black individual—particularly a black female—growing up under a Jim Crow regime may mean acquiescing to the control of social realities. Cora quickly concludes that "it's gonna be awful hard to be a colored woman" (*Walk,* 73). Her life and the lives of other blacks whom she encounters allow for a "complex and sustained examination of individuals struggling with the conflicting demands of private need and public commitment" (Walker, 91) and the ways in which unresolved tensions between the two impede true personal fulfillment.

Childress draws on a variety of devices to unify *A Short Walk.* In framing the novel with birth and death—starting with the birth of Cora and the passing of her birth mother and concluding with Cora's own demise—Childress stresses the cyclicity of human existence from the cradle to the grave. The first 10 chapters, set in Charleston, cover the first two decades of Cora's life, focusing on her intellectual maturation, her adoptive father's death, and her marriage to and subsequent abandonment of the unctuous Kojie Anderson. Excepting a few episodes—Cora's two-month excursion to Cuba, Central America, and Jamaica on the inaugural voyage of Marcus Garvey's the SS *Frederick Douglass,* her tours as a minstrel performer throughout the South, and the death of her adoptive mother on Edisto Island—the remaining 19 chapters are set in Harlem.

In place of dating the novel's episodes by years, Childress's passing allusions to significant historical events denote specific points in time. Drawn with great accuracy, the heyday of minstrelsy, the World Wars, prohibition, the rise and fall of Marcus Garvey, the stock market crash of 1929, and the Harlem riot of 1943 locate Cora in a colorful period. Indeed, much of the historical authenticity of *A Short Walk* is lost on the reader unfamiliar with the era of the Harlem Renaissance. Childress bases a large portion of the Garvey material and smaller bits of local details on historically documented data. For example, the name Cora Green (Cora's name after she marries her childhood sweetheart, Cecil Green) was that of a real-life actress who was a part of the Harlem scene at its pinnacle (Walker, 214). Other embedded allusions throughout the narrative, such as that of "Butterbeans and Susie," an early minstrel team, and the black-organized Improved Benevolent Protective Order of Elks of the World, the first chartered Elk order, exemplify Childress's persistent weaving of the factual with the fictional.

Alternating the narration of the story between a third-person omniscient, present-tense point of view and Cora's spontaneous, colloquial first-person, present-tense accounts gives the novel immediacy and dramatic stage direction. Two distinct narrators also provide dual vantage points from which to process details. As in the multivocality of Childress's adolescent fiction, Cora and the omniscient narrator sometimes confirm and sometimes contradict but always complement each other.

The emergence of Cora's narrative voice at the beginning of chapter 5 coincides with the end of her eighth-grade year and the commencement of her menses, her biological induction into womanhood. About 13 years old, Cora is at the juncture where she may bring new life into the world and to supply new direction to her own. Inscribed in her first observations is an awakening ability to assess situations and to link causes with effects, a skill that will later be essential to her survival as a single woman on the streets of Harlem. She connects her family's increasing poverty with the war overseas, which "somehow . . . makes things more high-priced here. Hard times are harder for us Negroes" (*Walk,* 75).

The omniscient narrator's follow-up report that blacks hope the United States will declare war on Germany so "those who go overseas will leave jobs open for those not going" indicates that an influx of immigrants has taken jobs previously held by blacks (*Walk,* 81). Oftentimes, however, "Cora's imagined version of the past is different from that reported by an omniscient and presumably reliable narrator." Learning of her white biological father, Cora concludes that he was "low-down" because he ran off leaving her mother pregnant. Reversing her conclusion, the omniscient narrator describes her white father as a young man caught in the throes of newly discovered passion but controlled by racist parents who sent him away (Walker, 91).

Folk expressions and myths contribute to the novel's authenticity as a slice of twentieth-century African American life and discourse. Proverbial wisdom, such as "Every shut-eye ain't sleep and every good-bye ain't gone" (*Walk*, 68), and clever one-liners, such as "Clean as the board a health" (meaning one is disease-free or dressed immaculately [*Walk*, 267]), are witticisms that still find their way into black folk speech. The folk beliefs that a cat can steal a person's breath and that "scrubbin [floors] toward the street door" in a house where the dead lie in state will drive away evil spirits that might claim the soul (*Walk*, 103) contribute fascinating nuggets of myth, ritual, and superstition to a narrative already rich in stimulating characters and details.

Life as a Minstrel Show

Cora's introduction to the race, class, and gender restrictions she will combat throughout her life comes on her fifth birthday. Cora learns from her adoptive father, Bill, as they walk to a production of Rabbit Ears Minstrel Show that life is "a short walk from the cradle to the grave," which they are walking "right this very minute" (*Walk*, 25). On this special day, Bill has told Cora she can do anything she wants, and she chooses, unknowingly, to defy Jim Crow law and enter the "white only" public park to admire its flowers. They make a hurried, unnoticed entrance, but are intercepted by a white policeman in the midst of Bill's attempt to hasten an undetected retreat. The policeman strips Bill of his human dignity before his young daughter, and Cora discovers that to the white world she is defined as "nigger." The incident compels Bill to explain the politics of living Jim Crow to Cora:

> Five is young but it's time for you to know that white folks got the law on their side. They can and do jail us, they can even lynch. . . . killin and murder, and hangin from trees, settin bodies afire. . . . We the colored, that's why he say "niggeras"; they the white, why we say "crackers." The rich white man run the courthouse, the bank, the jobs . . . and the poor white cracker is mean cause he don't run nothin and is scared we gonna cut him outta what little he do get holda. They glad for any excuse to kill us off. (*Walk*, 29)

The configuration of the Rabbit Ears Minstrel Show audience mirrors the hierarchies her father describes. Blacks sit on the far sides of the tent, separated from whites. Poor whites sit front and center, while well-to-do whites sit behind them, "amused by the audience as well as the show" (*Walk*, 35). The segregated seating does not, however, prevent black women and white men from conducting clandestine communications. Cora "begins to decipher the true language of their world . . . behind the cross-currents of looks and laughter" as black prostitutes drop small cards that white men secretly scoop up (*Walk*, 36).

Onstage, as well as behind its scenes, the minstrel show is white owned and run. The production "might be *called* a colored minstrel and colored might be in it, but who you think pocket the money?" Cora overhears Bill soberingly remind another black patron (*Walk*, 31). Wearing a top hat, the "best suit a clothes and a diamond ring" (*Walk*, 34), the white Mister Interlocutor, the top man of the show who never has to blacken his face, runs the traveling troupe, making all of its onstage decisions. He directs all the black actors, who are in blackface to exaggerate their dark complexion, and he "asks all the questions and gets all the answers. . . . calls the tune and says who is to speak, dance or sing" (*Walk*, 34). Offstage, he determines the professional careers of the blacks in his employment. When white resistance to the beautiful Rosalinda, played by Cora's Aunt Francine, singing a dignified light opera tune on the subject of freedom sets off a riot, the white director dismisses Francine and her husband from the company.

In real life, as in the slapstick onstage, whites expect blacks to act the part of buffoons, like Chief Boo Roo of Kookalanki and his big-bottomed daughter, Ross-a-jass. The image of the lovely Rosalinda, singing in a "clear, sweet soprano: 'Let them be free, let them be free; Oppression, dear father, is slavereeee' . . ." (*Walk*, 42), jars whites' sexually defined notion of the black woman. Her sole role onstage is to shake and shimmy, flaunt herself seductively for their sensual amusement. Rosalinda's refinement and the broader social implication of the song, which within the context of the sketch pleads for Rastus and Mister Bones's freedom from a stew pot but metaphorically doubles as a plea for racial equality, threatens white hegemony.

On multiple levels, Cora surmises by the end of her "short walk" that "the 'minstrel' is not confined to a tent" (*Walk*, 215). In contradistinction to her father's definition of life, she concludes from her own observations that it is "a damned first-class minstrel show" and that she has "been sittin front row center all the way" (*Walk*, 325). In accordance with the politics of living Jim Crow, which a minstrel life dictates, Cora learns as early as five not to act herself but to negotiate racial survival by taking cues from older experienced blacks such as her father, who sacrifice portions of their dignity every day to stay alive.

When Will Rosalinda Sing?

The riotous culmination of the Rabbit Ears Minstrel episode poses a fundamental question about the uncertain artistic futures of black professional actors and actresses whose roles at the beginning of the twentieth century were confined to slapstick and raunchy comedy routines. When blacks staged serious dramas, resentful whites often opposed their ambitions to high culture. In some instances, white opposition took violent form. In her introduction to *Black Scenes* (1971), Childress documents an early example of such resistance to a black Shakespearean production, which served as a historical precedent on which to base the Rosalinda episode:

> In 1823 the free Blacks of New York City opened a theatre at what is now Bleecker and Grove Streets in Greenwich Village. James Hewlett, a West Indian, was the founder. The company performed Shakespearean drama. The white press and some of the public resented these Africans performing *Richard III*. A mob protested by pelting them with rocks. The company was arrested, jailed, and warned that in the future they must limit themselves to material more suitable to their station in life.[4]

Similarly pelted with cups, spoons, and half-eaten food, Rosalinda of the minstrel sketch is sent the message in no uncertain terms that whites perceive her as "uppity" and out of her "place." Childress constructed the Rosalinda scene and the ensuing riot to frame the unanswered question, "When will Rosalinda sing?" (*Walk,* 206). Restated, the question asks when will the moment come that black actors and actresses can do what is not comic or raunchy or ridiculous without white opposition, restriction, or control.

Cora's awe of her Aunt Francine's talent and beauty inspires her to become a Rosalinda. Encouraging her aspiration, Francine says that "[a]ll girls have a Rosalinda inside of them; she's there waiting to sing or teach school, to do something fine before the world" (*Walk,* 48). But the impenetrable wall of racism thwarts the artist budding inside Cora.

Some time later, after whites object to the "political" nature of a freedom pageant scheduled for performance at Cora's church and invite themselves to review its contents, the congregation cancels the pageant, substituting a "My Determination" program. Deference to meddling whites upsets Cora, who had planned to dramatize a scene from *A Midsummer Night's Dream* as Titania for the pageant. She is reduced to reciting "a poem or a verse from scripture, then end by sayin, 'I'm a child a Gawd and my determination is to serve him in life as a . . . cook, baby nurse, or some such, . . . and help enlighten and uplift my people.'" Participation in the "My Determination" program, a type of inverted minstrel show that concedes to whites' definition of blacks' "place," is abhorrent to Cora, who argues that "Times oughta change" (*Walk,* 70).

Nevertheless, she accedes to her mother's counsel to bide her time by placing a "latch" on her mouth and silencing her ideas (*Walk,* 73). The incident silences the Rosalinda in Cora and foils her opportunity to do some fine thing before the world. In her adulthood, Cora's talents as a card sharp in New York and as a traveling performer throughout the South afford a margin of creative release but do not provide serious and satisfying opportunities for the true artist in her.

Men, Identity, and Ownership

Cora bonds early with Bill James, who advises direct resistance to racism, in contrast with her mother Etta, who counsels resignation and patience. It is his paternal guidance that she credits as the source of her "mannish ideas" (*Walk,* 187). Dying slowly of diabetes, her father bequeaths her his only legacy, his wisdom and the encouragement to be autonomous. Bill counsels Cora that her mind is the only one she will "have for full time use" (*Walk,* 101) and that she is just as capable as Kojie Anderson, whom most consider the smartest and most industrious black man in town. Liberal in his views, Bill does not minimize the potential of Cora's life because of her gender. He instructs Cora that her future options are not limited to marriage and childbearing. Achieving self-reliance through education or skill in a trade is an equally fine choice. "When I'm gone," he requests of Cora, "please go to the old slave market and address yourself to it, say, 'That's all you gonna get, my father is the last. I'll be no man's slave, I belong to myself'" (*Walk,* 101). To his stirring words, Cora pledges that she will learn to earn her "own livin without a bossman" (*Walk,* 101).

Bill also tells Cora that he and Etta are not her biological parents, leaving her with an uncertain sense of identity and family connection. An earlier encounter with Mountain Seeley, a faith healer who takes her money and sexually exploits her, teaches Cora that being a woman is more than experiencing her first menstrual period; "it's bein afraid, alone and not knowin the true from the false, or whose word to take" (*Walk,* 98). Now the news of her adoption points out that reality is not always a neatly fixed property; even being a daughter is a state of being subject to change. The sudden destabilization of her identity leads to uneasy feeling that she "belong[s] to nobody atall" (*Walk,* 104), despite her father's assurance that she belongs solely to herself. From the time of her father's death to the end of her life, self-possession and self-determination—"livin without a bossman"—remain Cora's most elusive goals.

Marriage to Kojie Anderson, a man noted for his "white" jailhouse job and unfailing pronunciation of the suffix "ing," reduces Cora to servitude. Although her affections lie with her childhood sweetheart Cecil Green, who flees Charleston under threat of white violence, she respects Kojie's education and progressiveness. Their marriage ostensibly offers security and the much sought after miracle that will keep her from moving to isolated Edisto Island with her mother after her father dies. She convinces herself that their union, an answer to her prayer, has somehow been providentially ordained.

On their wedding day, Kojie escorts Cora to the door of her new home as if she were a prisoner being led to a cell. He grips her arm, "not even lettin go while he searches his pockets for keys" (*Walk,* 119). Once inside, his oscillation between explaining the endless rules of his militaristic household and fondling of her nipples and crotch through her clothing reveals that he sees her primarily as a cross between domestic servant and sexual object. She is the newest furnishing for his five-room house, which is equipped with running water. Her value to him resides in her youth, purity, beauty, and submissiveness. That she is unspoiled sexual goods is of utmost importance. Before consummating their marriage, Kojie humiliatingly inspects Cora's genitals by lamplight, "asking a flood of questions" to dispel any apprehension that she has had sexual relations with a man or a woman (*Walk,* 126). Free of stretch marks, her "smooth as silk" belly and thighs convince him that she has never given birth (*Walk,* 127). Following their first coupling, he rolls her over to certify that the blood providing proof of a ruptured hymen is present. Kojie's treatment of his new bride resembles a slave owner's crude physical examination of his newly purchased human chattel.

A literal prisoner in her own house, a lonely Cora follows Kojie's order not to socialize often with other blacks in the community because "too many niggers" get on his nerves (*Walk,* 121). Careful to keep her financially dependent, Kojie never gives Cora money unless he knows for what purpose it will be spent. Like Janie Crawford in her vacuous marriage to Logan Killicks in Hurston's *Their Eyes Were Watching God,* Cora cannot emotionally commit herself to a true conjugal union with Kojie, who wants her to be jealous of his deceased first wife to prove her adoration of him. For Cora, sex between them is little more than an out-of-body experience: "Some nights it seems as if she is standing aside in a corner of the bedroom, watching Kojie and Cora Anderson struggling through their evening connections. She listens to his sounds and cries, hearing her own voice trying to match them. Her body is there in the bed with him, but she is gone—to the corner of the room, high up near the ceiling," where she plans the next day's meal or chore (*Walk,* 130).

Kojie's jealousy makes him a wife beater. Her kindness to the black prisoners of a chain gang repairing the curbstone outside their home precipitates Kojie's first—and last—beating of Cora. She gives the men water and pie, but Kojie believes that what they really want is a piece of her. He sees her innocent gesture as a means of ridiculing him, thereby sanctioning his violence. A further source of his violence is the physical abuse he witnessed as a child between his parents. Just as his father did with his mother, Kojie has Cora hold onto a pot lid while he beats her, striking her in places where the bruises will not be exposed to public scrutiny. Invoking the myth that black women are innately loose sexually justifies his abuse. Actually, Kojie imputes to the men of the chain gang his own sexual objectification of Cora, never seeing beyond that to acknowledge her personhood and right to autonomy. Kojie covets Cora as a possession marked with his brand: "Your name is Anderson, bitch!" he corrects her when she resists his ugly accusation that she is a "cock-teaser" by stating, "My name is Cora James and my determination is to be respected." Seeing her as his prized animal, Kojie accuses the men of the chain gang of wanting to get into his "stall" to take what is his (*Walk,* 135).

With all pretensions that fate brought them together gone, Cora silently submits that for security's sake she attached herself to a loveless marriage, "coveting Kojie Anderson's house and pay envelope" and "using him to keep from going to Edisto Island" (*Walk,* 128). The remembrance that she does have options, that she "ain't no slave," and that she belongs to herself (*Walk*, 138) empowers Cora to leave her stifling, abusive marriage to Kojie and head for New York and another life.

In stark contrast to the compulsive possessiveness of Kojie, Cecil Green, with whom Cora is reunited during her second year in Harlem, is a male chauvinist possessed by sociopolitical ideologies. An ardent follower of Marcus Garvey and supporter of the Universal Negro Improvement Association (UNIA), an organization that leaves little room for attending to his personal needs, Cecil writes for its newspaper, *Negro World*. Through Cecil, Cora's black consciousness and her self-consciousness are raised. Gaining knowledge of "the poor of the West Indies, the histories of the Afro-Americans, The African Orthodox Church, the plight of South American cane cutters," and Garvey's determination to liberate blacks from whites by returning them to Africa (*Walk*, 165), Cora gains insight into black accomplishments and oppression worldwide.

After prolonged exposure to the UNIA, Cora notes how its blatant sexism marginalizes women. The organization appoints Laverne Washington, who sells more UNIA stock than anyone, to the post of nurse on the ship *Black Star Line* and gives her free passage on its maiden voyage as her reward, but it does not offer her a cabinet position. Cora volunteers to accompany Cecil in meetings aboard ship as a secretary, but he tells her that the ship's business is men's business, requiring men's intellectual prowess: "No other women will be there. You wouldn't understand it," he insultingly explains (*Walk*, 192). In sum, Cecil expects Cora to be content with serving as his ornament at social functions, such as dinners at the captain's table and the ball at the presidential palace in Havana.

Cecil's commitment to a social movement that denies women equal participation on the one hand and demands his total devotion on the other leaves little opportunity for Cora to integrate herself into his public sphere or Cecil to enter into her private space. Cora, who idealistically wants "to settle down to true love, the kind you read about in storybooks" (*Walk*, 250), wants Cecil to love her as much as he loves the black nationalist movement. But Cecil believes that "there's little room for love until we solve this race hell" (*Walk*, 240). The failure of Garvey's *Black Star Line* to stay financially afloat because of its managers' lack of business acumen and Garvey's deepening government entanglements inevitably sabotage any chance they might have had to revive their youthful romance. Pressure to save the voyage from financial ruin and himself from imprisonment evokes Cecil's criticism of what he perceives to be Cora's failure to appreciate his position, although he never offers up explanations.

Cora will not be Cecil's whipping post and shadow, asking, "Why do I have to agree just to halfway get along?" (*Walk,* 213). Cecil's support of Garvey's racist policies further erodes her respect for the rival of his affections and her tie with the movement. The movement's engulfment of Cecil, its denouncement of all whites, and its allegiance with the Klan in advocating total segregation lead Cora to wonder whether she is "walking away from the Black Nationalist Movement" or if "it's walking away from me" (*Walk,* 222).

A true test of the conflicting demands of private need and public commitment arises when Cora announces to Cecil, once they return to the states, that she is pregnant with their child. In his preoccupation with the movement, he fails to comprehend the significance of her announcement. Thus "even fatherhood does not move him toward private life. For Cora, however, pregnancy means that she must shift again from rebel to survivor; when she considers her options and thinks about how she will take care of a baby, she quickly concludes that 'money is the answer'" (Walker, 95).

The financial demands of approaching single motherhood dictate Cora's private choice to team up with Napoleon Ramsey (Nappy). Prior to her reunion with Cecil, Cora had a brief affair with Nappy, a frequenter of her cousin Estelle's parties for select black gentlemen. Nappy, who teaches her the art of card dealing and parts of his comedy routines, offers Cora yet another kind of relationship with a male. First, he is not sexually possessive. Cora's intimate involvement with Cecil ignites no jealousy, and he considerately volunteers to pretend that he is the father of her baby. Second, he is neither politically possessed nor publicly committed. A pragmatist, Nappy preaches that "[o]ur people have to first make a livin and take care a the race problem later" (*Walk,* 157). Foremost, Nappy concerns himself with his personal interests. He demands no exclusive sexual right to Cora but does expect sexual privilege—"a soft bosom to lay his head on [come] night" (*Walk,* 241).

Cora's shifting allegiances to these three men and later to a fourth, the white Simeon, reflect her efforts to come to terms with her social and political beliefs. First with Kojie she attempts a satisfying private life of domestic bliss, but spousal domination and sexual objectification suffocate the marriage. She then steps into the public arena to protest racial inequities. Joining with Cecil, she boycotts white businesses that refuse to hire blacks. Staging her own protest, she threatens a riot on a Jim

Crow train if her demand for access to dining-car service is not met. To weather the Depression, during which Nappy's philosophy "to first make a livin" outweighs the need to address the race problem and resist white control, she teams up with Simeon, who sets her up as proprietor of an illegal gambling house. None of these stances offers Cora lasting fulfillment, since singularly none of them provides a sustaining political and spiritual fullness.

Cora considers herself just as much or even more of a black nationalist than Cecil, whose public position as a separatist and a nationalist are inconsistent with his personal life. After Garvey's Africa campaign fails, Cecil affiliates himself with the Harlem Labor Union as a street speaker educating the public on the power of boycotts, petitions, and the picketing of City Hall. Talking black but sleeping white, he takes a white woman as a mistress but hides her from public view. In contrast, Cora's inability, despite her best efforts, to give herself wholly to Simeon underscores her deep-seated racial allegiance. She reflects, "I don't preach on the street corner, but my nationalism is right here in this room" (*Walk,* 312). Cora transcends the passive compliance of the preceding black generation by becoming racially assertive and interracially cooperative with Simeon. Nevertheless, private issues of racism and racialized behavior insist that she reserve true intimacy for those who share her black ancestry.

Cora's concession to accompany Cecil as his wife on the maiden voyage of the *Frederick Douglass* to Cuba while she is still legally married to Kojie is intended to prove that some part of her belongs to herself despite what the government mandates. Yet the trip to the West Indies reveals that there is still much of herself in need of reclamation. The pretense of marriage and the assumption of Cecil's name threaten her identity. "There's no big to-do about a *man's* name. For the rest of your life you'll walk around with the one you were born with, always knowin exactly who you are from one end of your life to the other. You are forever Cecil Green. My real mother was Johnson, she died and I became 'James,' then Kojie turned me into 'Anderson.' Now you say 'Mrs. Green,' 'Lady Green'—I never seem to know who I am!" Cora complains (*Walk,* 180), citing the name changes and redefinings of self to which women are subjected throughout their lives.

Throughout her unfulfilling relationships with black men Cora never forgets that social causes and their traumatizing psychological effects are at work on them as well. It is this insight that allows her to empathize with them in the midst of their most denigrating treatments of her. As an adolescent, she perceives "that people's behavior is conditioned, if not determined, by public realities" (Walker, 93). A neighbor's brutal stabbing of his wife with an ice pick causes her to wonder "if it had to do with not having money, or perhaps who slept with who, or maybe the price of oranges, or the colored and white signs . . . or some such thing" (*Walk,* 91). She similarly discerns that Kojie made her "pay . . . in strange hurtful ways" for the "iron hand of the white man" upon him (*Walk,* 187), and that the privately detached Cecil, to a large degree, is a product of the socially conflicted times in which he lives.

Gender Ideologies

A Short Walk elaborates on the male devaluation of black women in a patriarchal society. Cora and her racial sisters cope through anger and acquiescence.

The words of Cora's mother ring true: "[E]very man wants to be the only sex part in a woman's life. Even if he goes with every woman in the world, he wants to be the first for each one" (*Walk,* 171). Subscribing to a double standard, men such as Kojie and Cecil sit in judgment of women who engage in uncommitted sex, though they are the men who make possible these casual sexual exchanges. Cora's virginity, dark brown hair, hazel eyes, and coffee-and-cream complexion make her a more valuable acquisition for Kojie, who has on occasion sought the relief of whores in Squeeze Gut Alley. Propositioning women in the church proved too humiliating and left him at a disadvantage when they bartered sex for marriage. Cecil accuses Cora of having lost her womanhood as well as her mind by consorting with Nappy, since Cecil expects "a woman to be a lady, whatever her color or position in life" (*Walk,* 241). Cora contests his pious sentiment, dismissing it as "A goddam lie!" She challenges him to "[l]ook in my eyes and tell the truth! . . . Have you ever in life gone to a place where you can buy a girl, just long enough to get some relief?" (*Walk,* 241). The stunning contradiction that he creates whores but does not want women to be whores shames him from meeting her gaze.

With no money to support Cora or their newborn daughter, Cecil cannot commiserate with Cora's selling her body to Nappy as a means of survival. "I did it for money," she explains. "My determination is to get out of any trouble I find myself in! I can't get anywhere on this streetcar called 'the world' without havin to pass some man who's always the conductor. And most of the time I have to pay my fare by layin out on the

flat a my back, just to get him to take me wherever he might be goin! . . .
No man gives anything away without a chance to get at some pussy!"
(*Walk*, 241).

White standards of beauty engender male rejection of black women
who are not a "tantalizin tan" or a "sun-kissed bronze" (*Walk*, 214).
Laverne, a "big-boned, stout . . . muddy brown" woman has "a harder
row to hoe . . . all because of the flesh" (*Walk*, 214). The highest seller of
Black Line stock and deemed a "fine, decent woman" (*Walk*, 242), she is
never chosen as a marriage partner because men cannot look beyond her
dark complexion and portliness to appreciate that she is a very agreeable
and spirited woman. Called "mammy" and "auntie" and depicted as the
butt of minstrel show jokes, women of Laverne's hue and stature are
denied male respect and companionship. When men stuff "balloons
beneath their clothes" and wear "big red bandanas to make sport of fat
black women . . . they ain't showin *me* to the world," Laverne contends,
"they're showin the world how *they* feel about me" (*Walk*, 215). In the
event that women of her physical description "somehow get married"
(*Walk*, 215), it is usually because "a wife is the only way a dirt-poor man
can get a lifetime servant, till death do part, to cook, clean and wait
upon him" (*Walk*, 215). In Kojie's beating of Cora, however, Childress is
quick to illustrate that although attractive women might be more readily sought after by men, they are equally likely to incur abuse.

Rage at sexual and racial exploitation crystallizes Cora's resistance to
male and white hegemony. Her father's instruction to "Hang onto
'mad'" (*Walk*, 100) in order not to succumb to a defeatist attitude with
respect to racism, and her extension of that advice in coping with
oppressive men, empower her verbal protests. A collective vision of
Mountain Seeley grabbing her breast while he pretends to offer healing
for her dying father, the white boys who threaten her with rape and
Cecil with death in the woods of Charleston, and "the eyes of Kojie peep-
ing at her private parts by lamplight" (*Walk*, 269) provokes Cora's voicing of rage on her final road tour. To the white manager who reneges on
his promise to pay advance money and then refuses her company accom-
modations fit for human occupancy because state law prohibits black
usage of white dressing rooms, Cora sounds off. "Fuck Georgia law, I
ain't made it! . . . And I ain't goin on without advance money. Call the
police if you wanta. Lettum come. Throw me in jail, lynch me—I'm
ready to die! This is my last stop on the Jim Crow line!" (*Walk*, 270). An
older, in-charge, but fed-up Cora knows exploitation in all its varied
forms and is now unafraid to call it out when it rears its ugly head.

Supportive Women

Apart from the men Cora continues to rely on, supportive women make up an indispensable part of her survival. Her New York cousin Estelle, the hostess of quiet respectable parties for Pullman porters and select theatrical people, sympathizes with Cora's departure from Kojie Anderson and unhesitatingly takes her into her Harlem home. A follower of the teachings of Christian Scientist Mary Baker Eddy, Estelle is an independent businesswoman living by mother wit and adhering to a woman's ideology even in her faith. Raising her daughter, Sugar, without male support, Estelle introduces Cora to tactical, practical methods of urban survival and self-employment at a time when black women, limited to menial labor and low wages, could expect employment only as mammies and maids in the homes of whites. Cora spends her first two years in Harlem working as a hostess and card dealer and learning the business end of Estelle's establishment.

Unhampered by race, Cora's friendship with May Palmas, who lives in Estelle's building, is a relationship wherein Childress explores interracial sisterhood without anger being an attendant feature. May, Cora's "first close girl-friend of any race" and her "closest friend since Papa died, . . . knows [like Bill James] how to look at matters and trace meanings and feelings down to the core" (*Walk,* 159). She also knows the pain of discrimination. Her "mixed" marriage to Apolinario, a Filipino, has prompted her Irish Catholic mother to disown her.

Enjoying each other's friendship, they support each other through personal crisis. May serves as Cora's spokesperson at an abortion that the distraught Cora cancels after she has been strapped to the midwife's table. Cora foils May's attempt to asphyxiate herself after Apolinario's arrest on charges of theft. She later furnishes support in May's emotional and financial recovery in his absence. During May's hospital rehabilitation, Cora claims her as family when May's mother persists in castigating her daughter's love for Apolinario. Their sisterhood proves to Cora that not all white people are hateful and that each must be judged individually "accordin to how they act, not by how they look" (*Walk,* 294).

Besides learning from Estelle how to survive in hard times, Cora also appropriates Estelle's sisterly generosity for the women she befriends and employs. Rescuing Laverne from the Bronx slave market, a Third Avenue pickup for black women seeking day work, Cora inducts her as blood kin: "You can help me take care of my little girl, help my poor, weary cousin Estelle. You must be family with us, sit down when you're tired, eat when you're hungry—we can share together" (*Walk*, 262). A mentally ill Laverne is no less a part of her family. Committed to being her sister's keeper, Cora supports Laverne until her forgetfulness becomes a threat to the safety of the household. She pledges to take care of Laverne upon her release from the institution to which she must commit her.

The scarcity of acting jobs, dignified work, and nonwhite employers keeps Cora's minstrel show intact despite her physical exhaustion and need to be with her daughter at home. For the sake of Cecil's Aunt Looli and the other women she employs, who would be reduced to prostitution and other degrading work, Cora places their needs above her own for as long as she can.

Accepting of difference, Cora heaps no moral indictments or social judgments on those who differ from her in sexual orientation and lifestyle. Looli's intimation of a lesbian affair with a younger woman in Cora's minstrel company does not arouse her condemnation. Her sisterly affection also extends to the female-identified Marion, her gambling-house cook, whose crowning moment is winning the transvestite Hamilton Ball. Cora loans him the $250 to buy the winning costume and is there to share the limelight when he is awarded the title. It is a concerned Marion, reciprocating supportiveness, who chides Cora on New Year's Day, the final day of her life, for not adhering to a strict diet because of her hypertension, diabetes, and enlarged heart. Cued by a common sensibility, Marion cancels his party plans to celebrate the New Year with Cora after Cecil calls to cancel his date with her.

Cora's continued pursuit of private fulfillment precipitates her death. Cecil and Cora marry to give Delta her rightful paternal surname, but Cora is unsuccessful in securing Cecil's love and commitment. Cecil cancels his date with Cora because, as he states, a "coalition meeting" is scheduled (*Walk*, 330). The claim is highly suspect, since it is New Year's Day. In all likelihood he is planning to spend the evening with his white girlfriend. Still, it is Cora's unwillingness to revoke her love for the emotionally elusive Cecil that causes her collapse on the street. Childress ties Cora's chasing of a windblown postcard with the inscription "*I Love You No Matter Where I Am!*"—purchased for him on her way to meet Marion—with her death, suggesting that Cora's romantic pursuit of Cecil is damaging to her well-being. Cora staggers and falls, dying from a heart too big and a compulsive, self-destructive love.

Cora's Progress

The social progress that Cora makes during her short walk is difficult to appraise. As Melissa Walker posits, Cora's "walk was taken in fits and starts and never with the intention of staying constantly on the road." Such being the case, "[t]he degree of her involvement in protest and social movements varies under the influence of external events and the demands of her private life" (92).

From a private perspective, Cora measures her social progress by the expansion of life choices open to Delta that were closed to her. As a young girl living in Charleston, Cora had dreams very much like Delta of seeing the world. Books shaped her fantasies of a future far away, while white movies give Delta "glimpses of a life she's never known—a perfect life filled with unlimited chance for careers, wealth, homes, and first-class travel by plane, train, and cruising ships—the strong, firm, belief in endless possibilities, dreams now shaping her every decision" (*Walk,* 322). Working as a ship's cabin girl seemed a possible way of satisfying Cora's wanderlust, but she quickly discovered that there are only cabin boys. While Cecil, being a male, was free to flee the South as a worker aboard a ship, Cora's destiny was "to be linked to first one person, then another," for survival (*Walk,* 324–25). Now that it is possible for her daughter to live an autonomous life—earn a "livin without a bossman" by choosing a nontraditional career for a woman—the issue of race clouds Cora's empowerment of Delta.

Both Cecil and Cora resist Delta's becoming a Wave or a Wac, but for different reasons. Consistent with his sexist view that women not occupy public spheres, Cecil will not sign for the underage Delta to join the national defense, stating, "Army and Navy—that's for men. Servicemen call such girls 'Government-inspected meat'" (*Walk,* 324). Conversely, Cora sees World War II as "no different from the other called 'One.' It's a white folks' fight—and both sides are united against us . . . . Why should we care?" (*Walk,* 325). Recognizing that the restraints that impeded her life are encroaching on Delta's short walk, Cora, desiring her daughter to have freedoms she never had, gives Delta consent to lead her own life. "I'll sign the consent paper. . . . Yes. There's some progress in that. My daughter can now be a cabin girl, in a manner of speakin, wherein I could not. So be it" (*Walk,* 325).

Following her enlistment, Delta's group engages in "protesting discrimination" in the military (*Walk,* 329). "Much more than for her parents, history is on Delta's side. Coming of age during World War II, she becomes an activist at a time when organized efforts to change society are about to bear fruit. . . . Without consciously attempting to do so, Cecil and Cora have raised a child who is a pioneer in the civil rights movement" (Walker, 97). With yet another "forty years done pass," Delta's life will not "live easy" in the sense Mr. July prophesied, but in comparison with Cora, she will be able to fight openly the racism and sexism that her mother on too numerous occasions had to stare in the face and tolerate.

Chapter Six

"A Candle in a Gale Wind"

Alice Childress continued to create because writing for her was "a labor of love and also an act of defiance, a way to light a candle in a gale wind" ("Candle," 111). In the name of artistic integrity she defied the pressures of submitting to black self-effacement and the parochialism of many literary reviewers. Her ceaseless questioning of "censors," who as "critics" often "abuse the privilege of telling us what to see and hear because, unfortunately, they know little about what they evaluate—the human condition," compelled her to trust her own creative instincts.[1] She argued that mechanical, unfair, and unenlightened literary judges were prone to "attack a writer's finest instinct as well as the worst. . . . They ban four-letter words while seven, eight, or nine-letter words often offer more mental poison" ("Knowing," 8–9).

Summarily dismissed by many white critics, Childress noted the black critic's inability to close or place in the winner's circle a white play. In the black theater, she said, "black experience has been fought against by white critics" who assume that "universal" and "the best" are synonymous with "white." Since "the white critic feels no obligation to prepare himself to judge a black play," he "simply has to ask himself, 'Did it strike me? Did I enjoy it? . . . If I could interchange these black characters for white, would this story apply to white people? If not, then I don't like it.'" Too often, the white writer, actor, and director respond to blacks' difficulties of getting their plays produced with, "'Well, it's hard for *me* to get work produced!'" Their egoism translates as "'I'm white and I can't. If I can't, what the hell do *you* expect?' That is to say, as long as there is a good white play that's not being done, we shouldn't complain" (Betsko and Koenig, 72).

Childress drew little distinction between those critics biased against blacks writing for the theater and those inclined to marginalize women playwrights. Believing mainstream theater to be exclusively male, many critics, she maintained, worked against a woman creating a great play since they were "threatened by the prospect of a strong point of view publicly expressed by a woman. . . . There's always resistance to any oppressed group, and this resistance stems from defensiveness: 'I fear your reaction to an unjust situation, so I must deny that it exists. I fear that advantages for you will threaten me.'" Therefore, these naysayers "must then claim that we have no fight—and say: 'There's nothing about your problem that's different from mine!'" (Betsko and Koenig, 72–73). Childress dismayingly acknowledged that some women critics, "the crafty ones . . . haven't allowed their minds to go beyond their own lives" and "have simply no ideas about the condition of other women. . . . It's amazing they can't see a broader picture and say, 'Well, maybe I've been very fortunate.' There'll always be a few women who will be Uncle Toms or a more sophisticated version of the same idea. Kowtowing to the one who is holding them down. Being Master's and Mistress's favorite child" (Betsko and Koenig, 73). Her own experiences as an appraiser of others' work—she served on Tony Award committees—taught her that other human factors also affect the critical response. Often critics are forced to see a play when they are tired, angry, or turned off by the subject matter.

Because trends of black self-censorship have been, at times, more problematic than marginalization and erasure by others, Childress fervently opposed the practice of racial self-effacement. She cautioned young writers to "be wary of those who [citing datedness or the unpleasantness of racial history] tell you to leave the past alone and confine yourselves to the present moment" ("Woman Playwright," 76). Furthermore, she asserted that as "long as we [blacks] are subliminally trained to recognize other racial feelings above our own, our ideas are in danger of being altered even before they are written. It becomes almost second nature to be on guard against the creative pattern of our own thought. Shall I ease in this bit of truth or that? Perhaps I can make a small point in the midst of a piece of nonsense" ("Candle," 114). She stated that self-censorship disguised as "pointless diatribes against ourselves"—criticizing low black voter turnout or Black English—detracts from the writer taking even the least progressive action. Conversely, Childress frowned upon a black or feminist aesthetic that exclusively privileges the idealization of women. Just as writers should not be expected to lie to make a piece work for the audience or reader, women should not be "obligated to write glowing things about our mothers or sisters. This prevents us from discovering each other. . . . We have a right to be wrong. . . . Whatever concepts or ideas we have we must feel free to express them, regardless of whether we catch hell or praise" (Betsko and Koenig, 74, 73).

Childress tenaciously protected both her writings and her personal life from interlopers and profiteers. Believing that what the public knew of her personally was unimportant, she was unwilling to divulge details of private experiences. Inaccuracies concerning her birth year and early life have been printed, yet she felt no obligation to correct them. Particularly off-limits was discussion of her private and professional relationship and subsequent break-up with Alvin Childress, who played the good-natured, philosophical cab driver, Amos Jones, in the 1950s television series "Amos 'n' Andy." An early member of the ANT, Alvin Childress performed in several plays with Alice Childress, including *Anna Lucasta*, and collaborated with her on playwriting projects. She would confirm neither the year of their marriage nor the year of their divorce. A betrayal by a friend of more than 40 years doubly intensified her professional and personal reticence.

In February of 1987 Childress's *Moms: A Praise Play for a Black Comedienne*, a comedy-musical, opened at the Hudson Guild Theater for a month's run. Actress Clarice Taylor, whose ties with Childress extended back to the 1940s and the American Negro Theatre, starred in the title role. Taylor had commissioned Childress to write a stage play of the life of the celebrated comedienne Jackie "Moms" Mabley from research Taylor had gathered. Childress's jazz musician husband, Nathan Woodard, interpolated songs for the production.

In September of the same year Childress brought suit against Taylor for infringement of copyright and unfair competition, after Taylor staged a similar version of *Moms* in August at the Astor Place Theatre. The second production failed to credit Childress. In fact, the playbill attributed authorship to Ben Caldwell, whom Taylor alleged she enlisted to write a revised version from her original research when Childress was unavailable to do so. Taylor argued that "facts in history" and "the structure" of Mabley's life had provided the structure of the play.[2] Childress called the second production "definitely plagiarism . . . shuffled here and there . . . but essentially . . . the same format." She did concede to "distinct differences in tone": the second *Moms* was "almost anything for a laugh. Jokes I had not allowed were in the [Astor Place] play." The second production was "not a different concept," just "a different feeling" (Gussow, 13). After a protracted court battle, Childress prevailed in her suit.

In her final years, Childress was committed to writing about her maternal great-grandmother, Ani Campbell, who was born under slavery, as an inspirational prelude to writing about her own life. When many whites violated Lincoln's emancipation decree, the public pressure of a legal deadline—"Juneteenth," or Final Freedom Night, one year after the Emancipation Proclamation—finally liberated blacks that slavers still held as property. Draped in rags, a 12-year-old Ani, clueless as to the whereabouts of any of her relatives, was taken to the center of Charleston, South Carolina, and abandoned. Anna Campbell, a white woman, rescued her and offered her a home. In time Ani adopted the surname of her benefactress. Anna Campbell's son, a sailor, fathered a child by Ani and then took to the sea never to return. The product of their union, a baby girl who was named after the fearless mother Eliza in Harriet Beecher Stowe's *Uncle Tom's Cabin*, later became the beloved maternal grandmother and artistic mentor of Childress. Exploring the life of her paternal Scotch-Irish great-grandmother also was to have been a part of the project.

In a 1987 interview, Childress spoke candidly about her status as the "first" African American female playwright to tread both literary and theatrical grounds that had been traditionally male and primarily white: "I never was ever interested in being the first woman to do anything. I always felt that I should be the 50th or the 100th. Women were kept out of everything. It almost made it sound like other women were not quite right enough or accomplished enough, especially when I hear 'the first Black woman.' When people are shut out of something for so long, it seems ironic when there's so much going on about 'the first'" (Brown-Guillory 1987, 68). Rejecting the importance of "firsts," Childress considered it a moral obligation to protect the ground gained by the defiance of past and present literary pioneers. "We also have to feel a sense of gratitude and admiration for what others have done, for those who have paved the way for us, and who are doing it even *now* in our time. The person who says, 'I'm not a woman playwright,' or 'I'm not black, I'm a writer who happens to be black,' et cetera, is deluding herself" (Betsko and Koenig, 73–74).

Notes and References

Preface

1. Gayle Austin, "Alice Childress: Black Woman Playwright as Feminist Critic," *Southern Quarterly* 25 (1987): 53; Austin refers to Childress's professionally produced play *Gold through the Trees.*
2. Elizabeth Brown-Guillory, "Alice Childress: A Pioneering Spirit," *SAGE* 4 (Spring 1987): 67; hereafter cited in the text.
3. Trudier Harris, "Alice Childress," in *Dictionary of Literary Biography 38: Afro-American Writers after 1955, Dramatists and Prose Writers,* ed. Thadious M. Davis and Trudier Harris (Detroit: Gale, 1985), 68; hereafter cited in the text.

Chapter One

1. Alice Childress, "A Candle in a Gale Wind," in *Black Women Writers (1950–1980): A Critical Evaluation,* ed. Mari Evans (New York: Doubleday, 1984), 112; hereafter cited in the text as "Candle."
2. Alice Childress, NCTE Lecture, November 1992; hereafter cited in the text as NCTE Lecture.
3. Alice Childress, "But I Do My Thing," in "Can Black and White Artists Still Work Together?" *New York Times,* 2 February 1969.
4. Doris Abramson, *Negro Playwrights in the American Theatre: 1925–1959* (New York: Columbia University Press, 1969), 186; hereafter cited in the text.
5. Rosemary Curb, "Alice Childress," in *Notable Women in the American Theatre: A Biographical Dictionary,* ed. Alice M. Robinson, Vera Mowry Roberts, and Milly S. Barranger (New York: Greenwood Press, 1989), 127.
6. Trudier Harris, introduction, in *Like One of the Family . . . Conversations from a Domestic's Life,* by Alice Childress (Boston: Beacon Press, 1986), xxxiii; hereafter cited in the text.
7. John O. Killens, "The Literary Genius of Alice Childress," in *Black Women Writers,* 131; hereafter cited in the text.
8. Kathleen Betsko and Rachel Koenig, "Alice Childress," in *Interviews with Contemporary Women Playwrights,* ed. Kathleen Betsko and Rachel Koenig (New York: William Morrow, 1987), 63; hereafter cited in the text.
9. Alice Childress, "The Black Experience: Why Talk about That?" *Negro Digest* 16 (April 1967): 21.
10. Alice Childress, *Wedding Band: A Love/Hate Story in Black and White* (New York: Samuel French, 1973), 5; hereafter cited in the text as *Wedding Band.*

11.   The other books banned were Richard Wright's *Black Boy,* Langston Hughes's *Best Short Stories of Negro Writers,* Piri Thomas's *Down These Mean Streets,* Bernard Malamud's *The Fixer,* the anonymously published *Go Ask Alice,* Oliver LaFarge's *Laughing Boy,* Desmond Morris's *The Naked Ape,* Kurt Vonnegut's *Slaughterhouse-Five,* and Eldridge Cleaver's *Soul on Ice.* The ban was later lifted on *Laughing Boy* and partially on *Black Boy.*

12.   Jackie Brooks, "Musical Premiere Scheduled," *State,* 9 October 1977, 2E.

13.   Alice Walker, "A Walk through Twentieth-Century Black America," *Ms.,* December 1979, 46, 48.

14.   Geraldine Wilson, "A Novel to Enjoy and Remember," *Freedomways* 20 (1980): 101–2.

15.   Mel Gussow, "The Stage: 'Moms,'" *New York Times,* 10 February 1987.

Chapter Two

1.   Nancie Caraway, *Segregated Sisterhood, Racism, and the Politics of American Feminism* (Knoxville: University of Tennessee Press, 1991), 3. Caraway refers to "white racism" as the "unseen signifier . . . which has segregated Black and white feminists and silences the former."

2.   A majority of the white suffragists were against extending the vote to black women. White women liberationists of the 1960s, inviting black women to join *their* movement, failed to acknowledge differences in their feminist agenda based on race. For an extended discussion, see bell hooks [Gloria Watkins], *Ain't I a Woman, Black Women and Feminism* (Boston: South End Press, 1981); hereafter cited in the text.

3.   Carol Tavris, *Anger: The Misunderstood Emotion* (New York: Simon and Schuster, 1982), 45.

4.   Alice Childress, *Florence, Masses and Mainstream* 3 (October 1950): 34–47; hereafter cited in the text as *Florence.*

5.   Elizabeth Brown-Guillory, *Their Place on the Stage, Black Women Playwrights in America* (New York: Greenwood Press, 1988), 54; hereafter cited in the text.

6.   Samuel A. Hay, "Alice Childress's Dramatic Structure," in *Black Women Writers,* 119.

7.   Deborah E. McDowell, "New Directions for Black Feminist Criticism," in *The New Feminist Criticism,* ed. Elaine Showalter (New York: Pantheon Books, 1985), 194.

8.   Sue-Ellen Case, *Feminism and the Theatre* (New York: Routledge, 1988), 101; hereafter cited in the text.

9.   Alice Childress, *Trouble in Mind: A Comedy-Drama in Two Acts,* in *Black Theatre: A Twentieth-Century Collection of the Work of Its Best Playwrights,* ed. Lindsay Patterson (New York: Dodd, Mead, 1971), 134–74; hereafter cited in the text as *Trouble.*

10. Ralph Ellison, *Invisible Man* (New York: Vintage Books, 1972), 16.

11. In 1987, independent filmmaker Robert Townsend, with the help of the Samuel Goldwyn Company, released *Hollywood Shuffle,* a lampoon of the racism that informs casting practices and the bulk of screen images of blacks as street hustlers, pimps, and prostitutes. The motion picture *Mandingo* (1975) is the story of a male slave whose sexual exploitation by his white mistress brings about his death.

12. Alice Childress, "About Those Colored Movies," in *Like One of the Family . . . Conversations from a Domestic's Life* (Boston: Beacon Press, 1986), 125; hereafter cited in the text as *Like One.*

13. "Like One of the Family," "Listen for the Music," "If You Want to Get Along with Me," "The Pocketbook Game," "The Health Card," "Mrs. James," "I Liked Workin' at that Place," "Weekend with Pearl," "Sometimes I Feel So Sorry," "I Hate Half-Days Off," "Story Tellin' Time," "Inhibitions," "Pretty Sights and Good Feelin's," "On Leavin' Notes," "Interestin' and Amusin'," "Ain't You Mad?," and "Let's Face It."

14. Trudier Harris, *From Mammies to Militants, Domestics in Black American Literature* (Philadelphia: Temple University Press, 1982), 188.

15. Mildred violates spatial etiquette again by taking a seat opposite Billy Alabama, the distant cousin of her mistress, in "Let's Face It" (*Like One,* 182–89).

16. Trudier Harris, "I Wish I Was A Poet": The Character As Artist in Alice Childress's *Like One of the Family," Black American Literature Forum* 14 (1980): 25; hereafter cited in the text. Also see Harris's introduction to *Like One of the Family,* xvi.

17. Roger Abrahams, *Deep Down in the Jungle: Negro Narrative Folklore from the Streets of Philadelphia* (Chicago: Aldine, 1970), 58.

18. Helen Davis, "Laughter and Anger," *Masses and Mainstream* 9 (July 1956): 50–51.

19. Autherine Lucy sought admission to the all-white University of Alabama in 1952 but was not admitted until February 1956. She was forced from campus by racist mobs of students and others, later re-admitted, and finally expelled by the university, which eventually integrated in the early 1960s.

20. Alice Childress, "The Negro Woman in American Literature," *Freedomways,* 6 (Winter 1966): 14–19; reprinted as "A Woman Playwright Speaks Her Mind," in *Anthology of the American Negro in the Theatre: A Critical Approach,* ed. Lindsay Patterson (New York: Publishers Co., 1968), 75–79; hereafter cited in the text as "Woman Playwright."

21. Rosemary Curb, "An Unfashionable Tragedy of American Racism: Alice Childress's *Wedding Band," MELUS* 7 (Winter 1980): 59.

22. Catherine Wiley, "Whose Name, Whose Protection: Reading Alice Childress's *Wedding Band,*" in *Modern American Drama: The Female Canon,* ed. June Schlueter (Rutherford: Fairleigh Dickinson University Press, 1990), 185–86; hereafter cited in the text.

    23.   The influenza epidemic, which swept the country in 1918, left 11 million dead.

    24.   Houston A. Baker, Jr., *Blues, Ideology, and Afro-American Literature: A Vernacular Theory* (Chicago: University of Chicago Press, 1984), 183; hereafter cited in the text.

    25.   William H. Grier and Price M. Cobbs, *Black Rage* (New York: Basic Books, 1968), 62.

    26.   Zora Neale Hurston, *Their Eyes Were Watching God* (New York: Harper and Row, 1990), 14.

    27.   Marge Jennet Price-Hendricks, "The Roaring Girls: A Study of Seventeenth-Century Feminism and the Development of Feminist Drama," diss., University of California, Riverside, 1987, 194; hereafter cited in the text.

    28.   Victor Turner, *The Ritual Process, Structure and Anti-Structure* (Ithaca: Cornell University Press, 1977), 96–97.

Chapter Three

    1.   Larry Neal, "The Black Arts Movement," in *The Black Aesthetic,* ed. Addison Gayle, Jr. (New York: Anchor Books, 1972), 257.

    2.   Mance Williams, *Black Theatre in the 1960s and 1970s* (Westport, Conn.: Greenwood Press, 1985), 112–13.

    3.   E. Franklin Frazier, *Black Bourgeoisie* (New York: Free Press, 1957), 236, 235.

    4.   Daniel P. Moynihan, "The Negro Family: The Case for National Action" (Washington, D.C.: U.S. Government Printing Office, 1965); reprinted in *Black Matriarchy Myth or Reality,* ed. John H. Bracey, Jr., August Meier, and Elliott Rudwick (Belmont, Calif.: Wadsworth Publishing Co., 1971), 126–59. "On this score, it should be stressed that although the Moynihan report provides most elaborate statistical evidence on the physical datum, father-absence, the only *empirical* evidence presented on the psychological datum, husband's subordination to the wife, is one study conducted in Detroit in 1955." One interpretation of this study suggested that the black family was egalitarian, rather than matriarchal, in pattern. The study does not address psychodynamic motivations for aggression and submission. "Highly aggressive behavior within the family is sometimes regarded as a defense or reaction on the part of the Negro male to his inferior status. If both submission *and* ascendance can be regarded as indicators of the feeling of subordination, it is hard to see how the theory could ever be refuted." See pp. 191–92, note 4, of Bracey, Meier, and Rudwick.

    5.   Alice Childress, *Wine in the Wilderness,* in *Wines in the Wilderness: Plays by African American Women from the Harlem Renaissance to the Present,* ed. Elizabeth Brown-Guillory (New York: Praeger, 1990), 134; Childress's play hereafter cited in the text as *Wine.*

    6.   Guy de Maupaussant, "The Piece of String," in *The Tales of Guy de Maupaussant* (New York: Heritage, 1964), 3–9.

7. Alice Childress, *String,* in *Mojo and String* (New York: Dramatists Play Service, 1971), 47: hereafter cited in the text.

8. Janet Brown, *Feminist Drama: Definition and Critical Analysis* (Metuchen; N.J.: Scarecrow Press, 1979), 68; hereafter cited in the text.

9. Gayle Austin, *Feminist Theories for Dramatic Criticism* (Ann Arbor: University of Michigan Press, 1990), 90–91; hereafter cited in the text.

10. Alice Childress, *Mojo: A Black Love Story,* in *Mojo and String,* 13; hereafter cited in the text.

Chapter Four

1. Alice Childress, *A Hero Ain't Nothin' but a Sandwich* (New York: Putnam, 1973), 107; hereafter cited in the text as *Hero.*

2. Amiri Baraka [LeRoi Jones], "It's Nation Time," in *It's Nation Time* (Chicago: Third World Press, 1970), 21–24.

3. Kenneth L. Donelson and Alleen Pace Nilsen, *Literature for Today's Young Adults,* 3d ed. (Glenview, Ill.: Scott, Foresman, and Co., 1989), 22–32.

4. Miguel A. Ortiz, "The Politics of Poverty in Young Adult Literature," *Lion and the Unicorn* 2 (Fall 1978): 13; hereafter cited in the text.

5. Ed Bullins, "*A Hero Ain't Nothin' But a Sandwich,*" *New York Times Book Review,* 4 November 1973, 40.

6. Alice Childress, *The African Garden,* in *Black Scenes,* ed. Alice Childress (New York: Doubleday, 1971), 145.

7. Alice Childress, *Rainbow Jordan* (New York: Coward, McCann and Geoghegan, 1981); hereafter cited in the text as *Rainbow.*

8. Zena Sutherland, "Alice Childress," in *The Best in Children's Books: The University of Chicago Guide to Children's Literature 1979–1984* (Chicago: University of Chicago Press, 1984), 84.

9. Sandra Y. Govan, "Alice Childress's *Rainbow Jordan:* The Black Aesthetic Returns Dressed in Adolescent Fiction," in *Children's Literature Association Quarterly* 13 (Summer 1988): 72.

10. Anne Tyler, "Looking for Mom," *New York Times Book Review,* 26 April 1981: 52–53.

11. Alice Childress, *Those Other People* (New York: Putnam, 1989), 33; hereafter cited in the text as *People.*

Chapter Five

1. Melissa Walker, *Down from the Mountaintop, Black Women's Novels in the Wake of the Civil Rights Movement, 1966–1989* (New Haven: Yale University Press, 1991), 91, 90; hereafter cited in the text.

2. Joseph McLellan, "*A Short Walk,* Harlem in the '30s: A Society in Flux, and a Heroine Standing Firm and Taming the Fury," *Washington Post* 28 December 1979.

3. Alice Childress, *A Short Walk* (New York: Coward, McCann and Geoghegan, 1979), 16; hereafter cited in the text as *Walk.*

4. Alice Childress, introduction, in *Black Scenes,* x.

Chapter Six

1. Alice Childress, "Knowing the Human Condition," in *Black Literature and Humanism,* ed. R. Baxter Miller (Louisville: University Press of Kentucky, 1981), 9; hereafter cited in the text as "Knowing."

2. Mel Gussow, "Theater Colleagues Dispute Authorship of 'Moms,'" *New York Times,* 18 August 1987.

Selected Bibliography

PRIMARY SOURCES

Young Adult Novels

A Hero Ain't Nothin' but a Sandwich. New York: Coward, McCann and
    Geoghegan, 1973.
Rainbow Jordan. New York: Coward, McCann and Geoghegan, 1981.
Those Other People. New York: G. P. Putnam's Sons, 1989.

Adult Novel

A Short Walk. New York: Coward, McCann and Geoghegan, 1979.

Anthologized Short Stories

Like One of the Family . . . Conversations from a Domestic's Life. Brooklyn, N.Y.:
    Independence Publishers, 1956; Boston: Beacon Press, 1986.

Published Plays

The African Garden. In *Black Scenes,* edited by Alice Childress, 137–45. Garden
    City, N.Y.: Doubleday, 1971.
Florence: A One Act Drama. Masses and Mainstream 3 (October 1950): 34–47.
Let's Hear It for the Queen. New York: Coward, McCann and Geoghegan, 1976.
Mojo: A Black Love Story. Black World 20 (April 1971): 54–82.
Moms: A Praise Play for a Black Comedienne. New York: Flora Roberts, 1993.
String. New York: Dramatists Play Service, 1969.
Trouble in Mind: A Comedy-Drama in Two Acts. In *Black Theatre: A Twentieth-*
    Century Collection of the Work of Its Best Playwrights, edited by Lindsay
    Patterson, 135–74. New York: Dodd, Mead, 1971.
Wedding Band: A Love/Hate Story in Black and White. New York: Samuel French,
    1973.
When the Rattlesnake Sounds. New York: Coward, McCann and Geoghegan,
    1975.
Wine in the Wilderness: A Comedy-Drama. In *Plays by and about Women,* edited by
    Victoria Sullivan and James Hatch, 379–421. New York: Vintage, 1973.
The World on a Hill. In *Plays to Remember,* edited by Henry B. Maloney, 103–25.
    Toronto: Macmillan, 1970.

Unpublished Plays

The Freedom Drum. Retitled *Young Martin Luther King, Jr.* Performing Arts
   Repertory Theatre, on tour 1969–72.
Gold through the Trees. New York, Club Baron Theatre, 1952.
Hell's Alley. With Alvin Childress, 1938.
Just a Little Simple. Adapted from Langston Hughes's collection *Simple Speaks His
   Mind.* New York, Club Baron Theatre, September 1950.
A Man Bearing a Pitcher (date unknown).
Sea Island Song. Charleston, South Carolina, Stage South, 1977. Retitled *Gullah.*
   Amherst, University of Massachusetts, 1984.

Screenplay

A Hero Ain't Nothin' but a Sandwich. New World Pictures, 1978.

Televised Productions

String. "Vision." PBS, 1979.
Wedding Band. ABC, 1973.
Wine in the Wilderness. "On Being Black." Boston, WGBH, 4 March 1969.

Edited Work

Black Scenes. Garden City, N.Y.: Doubleday, 1971.

Articles and Essays

"Alice Childress." In *Speaking for Ourselves: Autobiographical Sketches by Notable
   Authors of Books for Young Adults,* edited by Donald R. Gallo, 39–40.
   Urbana: NCTE, 1990.
"The Black Experience: Why Talk about That?" *Negro Digest* 16 (April 1967):
   17–21.
"Black Writers' Views on Literary Lions and Values." *Negro Digest* 17 (January
   1968): 36, 85–87.
"But I Do My Thing." "Can Black and White Artists Still Work Together?"
   New York Times, 2 February 1969.
"A Candle in a Gale Wind." In *Black Women Writers (1950–1980): A Critical
   Evaluation,* edited by Mari Evans, 111–16. New York: Doubleday, 1984.
"For a Negro Theatre." *Masses and Mainstream* 4 (February 1951): 61–64.
"Knowing the Human Condition." In *Black Literature and Humanism,* edited by
   R. Baxter Miller, 8–10. Louisville: University Press of Kentucky, 1981.
"The Negro Woman in American Literature." *Freedomways* 6 (Winter 1966):
   14–19. Reprinted as "A Woman Playwright Speaks Her Mind." In
   Anthology of the American Negro in the Theatre: A Critical Approach, edited
   by Lindsay Patterson, 75–79. New York: Publishers Co., 1968.

"The Soul Man." *Essence,* May 1971, 68–69, 94.
"Tribute—to Paul Robeson." *Freedomways* 2 (First Quarter 1971): 14–15.

Interviews

Betsko, Kathleen, and Rachel Koenig. "Alice Childress." In *Interviews with Contemporary Women Playwrights,* edited by Kathleen Betsko and Rachel Koenig, 62–74. New York: William Morrow, 1987.
Brown-Guillory, Elizabeth. "Alice Childress: A Pioneering Spirit." *SAGE* 4 (Spring 1987): 66–68.
"Conversation with Alice Childress and Toni Morrison." *Black Creation* 6 (1974–75): 90–92.
Maguire, Roberta. "Alice Childress," in *The Playwright's Art: Conversations with Contemporary American Dramatists,* edited by Jackson R. Bryer, 48–69. New Brunswick, N.J.: Rutgers University Press, 1995.

SECONDARY SOURCES

Articles and Parts of Books

Abramson, Doris E. *Negro Playwrights in the American Theatre: 1925–1959,* 168–70, 188–204, 258–60, 284. New York: Columbia University Press, 1969. A critical discussion of *Trouble in Mind* that argues that too much of the play "assault[s] race prejudice at every turn."
Anderson, Mary Louise. "Black Matriarchy: Portrayals of Women in Three Plays." *Black American Literature Forum* 10 (Fall 1976): 93–95. Asserts that in contrast to Lorraine Hansberry's *A Raisin in the Sun* and James Baldwin's *The Amen Corner,* which show how black women cope with their matriarchal qualities, Childress's *Wine in the Wilderness* illustrates how a black man learns to cope with the matriarchal stereotype.
Austin, Gayle. "Alice Childress: Black Woman Playwright as Feminist Critic." *Southern Quarterly* 25 (Spring 1987): 53–62. Summarizes Childress's career as social critic and reverser of male-constructed images of black women, then focuses on *Trouble in Mind* and *Wine in the Wilderness*'s movement through the three stages of feminist criticism as outlined by Elizabeth Abel.
———. *Feminist Theories for Dramatic Criticism,* 89–92. Ann Arbor: University of Michigan Press, 1990. Asserts that Childress as feminist critic gives the "sign of Woman" double cultural meaning in her depiction of Tomorrow Marie in *Wine in the Wilderness.*
Brown, Janet. *Feminist Drama: Definition and Critical Analysis,* 56–70. Metuchen, N.J.: Scarecrow Press, 1979. Argues that *Wine in the*

Wilderness is a feminist play since it depicts a female protagonist asserting her autonomy in opposition to an unjust sociosexual hierarchy.

Brown-Guillory, Elizabeth. "Black Women Playwrights Exorcising Myths." *Phylon* 48 (Fall 1987): 229–39. Credits Childress, Lorraine Hansberry, and Ntozake Shangé with dispelling the myths of "the contented slave," "the tragic mulatto," "the comic negro," "the exotic primitive," and "the spiritual singing, toe-tapping, faithful servant" created by black male and white playwrights. Their constructions include "the black militant," "the black peacemaker," "the optimistic black capitalist," "the struggling black artist," "the black male in search of his manhood," "the black male as walking wounded," and "the evolving black woman."

———. "Images of Blacks in Plays by Black Women." *Phylon* 47 (September 1986): 230–37. Compares the female protagonist's development in *Wine in the Wilderness* with six stages designated in Koine Greek (or the common man's Greek, spoken from the Hellenstic through the Roman periods): *koinonia* (communal fellowship), *logus* (confusion and doubt), *metanoia* (turning away), *kergyma* (compulsion to speak, lash out), *didache* (summation, formal message passed on to others), and *eucharistia* (combining inner wholeness with outer community).

———. *Their Place on the Stage: Black Women Playwrights in America.* Westport, Conn.: Greenwood Press, 1988. Summarizes and compares the work of Childress, Lorraine Hansberry, and Ntozake Shangé.

Curb, Rosemary. "Alice Childress," In *Dictionary of Literary Biography 7: Twentieth-Century American Dramatists,* edited by John MacNicholas, 118–24. Detroit: Gale Research Co., 1981. General summary of works and brief biographical information.

———. "An Unfashionable Tragedy of American Racism: Alice Childress's *Wedding Band.*" *MELUS: Journal for the Study of the Multi-Ethnic Literature of the United States* 7 (Winter 1980): 57–68. Discusses the repressive and unjust impact that "anti-woman" laws have on Childress's black women.

Davis, Helen. "Laughter and Anger." *Masses and Mainstream* 9 (July 1956): 50–51. Observes that *Like One of the Family,* rousing the reader to tears and laughter but mostly to anger, could be presented almost unchanged as dramatic monologues but makes the criticism that the conversations lack an unexpected point of view.

Govan, Sandra Y. "Alice Childress's *Rainbow Jordan:* The Black Aesthetic Returns Dressed in Adolescent Fiction." *Children's Literature Association Quarterly* 13 (Summer 1988): 70–74. Assesses *Rainbow Jordan* in terms of the essential tenets of the black aesthetic as defined by the black nationalist Maulana Ron Karenga: black art must be "functional," that is, "useful"; "collective . . . emerge from and return or speak to the people"; and "it must be 'committing' or committed."

Harris, Trudier. "Alice Childress." In *Dictionary of Literary Biography 38: Afro-American Writers after 1955, Dramatists and Prose Writers,* edited by Thadious M. Davis and Trudier Harris, 66–79. Detroit: Gale Research Co., 1985. General summary of works and brief biographical infor-mation.

————. "Beyond the Uniform: Alice Childress, *Like One of the Family* (1956)." In *From Mammies to Militants: Domestics in Black American Literature,* 111–33. Philadelphia: Temple University Press, 1982. Cites Mildred, the feisty domestic of *Like One of the Family,* as "a bridge between the transitional northern maids who espouse freedom of mind and the revolutionary maids who exhibit freedom of action."

————. "'I Wish I Was a Poet': The Character as Artist in Alice Childress's *Like One of the Family.*" *Black American Literature Forum* 14 (Spring 1980): 24–30. Discusses Childress's blending of European, White American, African, and African American written and oral traditions to create a narrative that allows the author total effacement and encourages participation between internal narrator and audience.

Hay, Samuel A. "Alice Childress's Dramatic Structure." In *Black Women Writers (1950–1980): A Critical Evaluation,* edited by Mari Evans, 117–28. New York: Doubleday, 1984. Examines the structure and symbolism of *Florence, Trouble in Mind,* and *Wine in the Wilderness.*

Hill, Elbert R. "A Hero for the Movies." In *Children's Novel's and the Movies,* edited by Douglas Street, 236–43. New York: Frederick Ungar, 1983. A comparison of the novel *A Hero Ain't Nothin' but a Sandwich* and its screenplay.

Holliday, Polly. "I Remember Alice Childress." *Southern Quarterly* 25 (Spring 1987): 63–65. Recounts Holliday's experiences of working with Childress and Joseph Papp in the New York Public Theater's 1972 production of *Wedding Band.*

Jennings, La Vinia Delois. "Alice Childress." In *Contemporary Poets, Dramatists, Essayists, and Novelists of the South,* edited by Robert Bain and Joseph Flora, 104–16. Westport, Conn.: Greenwood Press, 1994. Gives a biographical overview and discusses the thematic phases of Childress's works.

Killens, John O. "The Literary Genius of Alice Childress." In *Black Women Writers (1950–1980): A Critical Evaluation,* edited by Mari Evans, 129–33. New York: Doubleday, 1984. Critiques *Trouble in Mind, Like One of the Family, Wedding Band, A Hero Ain't Nothin' but a Sandwich,* and *A Short Walk.*

Mitchell, Loften. "Three Writers and a Dream." *Crisis* 72 (April 1965): 219–23. Along with the drama of William Branch and John Oliver Killens, outlines Childress's contributions as a playwright from *Florence* to *Wedding Band.*

Ortiz, Miguel A. "The Politics of Poverty in Young Adult Literature." *The Lion and the Unicorn* 2 (Fall 1978): 6–15. A review of *A Hero Ain't Nothin' but a*

Sandwich, concentrating on the ways in which social and economic circumstances affect the actions of characters.

Troutman-Robinson, Denise. "The Elements of Call and Response in Alice Childress' *Like One of the Family.*" *MAWA Review* 4 (June 1989): 18–21. Compares Mildred's conversations with the sermons of the preacher in the black oral tradition.

Walker, Alice. " A Walk through Twentieth-Century Black America." *Ms.* December 1979, 46–47. Praises *A Short Walk* for its authentic historical coverage but blames it for its "forced folksiness" and echoes of Ann Petry's Lutie Johnson in *The Street* and Zora Neale Hurston's Janie Crawford in *Their Eyes Were Watching God.*

Walker, Melissa. *Down from the Mountaintop: Black Women's Novels in the Wake of the Civil Rights Movement, 1966–1989,* 90–99. New Haven: Yale University Press, 1991. Asserts that the political issues that were at the forefront of the civil rights movement are interwoven in the 1930s–1940s plot of *A Short Walk.*

Wiley, Catherine. "Whose Name, Whose Protection: Reading Alice Childress's *Wedding Band.*" In *Modern American Drama: The Female Canon,* edited by June Schlueter, 184–97. Rutherford: Fairleigh Dickinson University Press, 1990. Points out the feminist movement's marginalization of black women while challenging that Childress's *Wedding Band* is less about interracial heterosexual relations than the absence of a sisterhood between black and white women.

Bibliographies

Arata, Esther Spring. *More Black American Playwrights: A Bibliography,* 57–59. Metuchen, N.J.: Scarecrow Press, 1978.

————, and Nicholas John Rotoli. *Black American Playwrights, 1800 to the Present: A Bibliography,* 46–49. Metuchen, N.J.: Scarecrow Press, 1976.

Campbell, Dorothy W. *Index to Black American Writers in Collective Biographies,* 63. Littleton, Colo.: Libraries Unlimited, 1983.

Curb, Rosemary. "Alice Childress." In *Notable Women in the American Theatre: A Biographical Dictionary,* edited by Alice M. Robinson, Vera Mowry Roberts, and Milly S. Barranger, 126–30. Westport, Conn.: Greenwood Press, 1989.

Eddleman, Floyd Eugene. *American Drama Criticism, Supplement III to the Second Edition,* 47–48. Hamden, Conn.: Shoe String Press, 1992.

Fairbanks, Carol, and Eugene A. Engeldinger. *Black American Fiction: A Bibliography,* 62. Metuchen, N.J.: Scarecrow Press, 1978.

French, William P., et al. *Afro-American Poetry and Drama, 1760–1975,* 259, 270, 273–74, 286, 353–55. Detroit: Gale Research Co., 1979.

Glikin, Ronda. *Black American Women in Literature: A Bibliography 1976 through 1987,* 26–28. Jefferson, N.C.: McFarland and Co., 1989.

Hatch, James Vernon, and Omanii Abdullah. *Black Playwrights, 1823–1977: An Annotated Bibliography of Plays,* 46–47. New York: Bowker, 1977.

Page, James Allen. *Selected Black American Authors: An Illustrated Bio-Bibliography Dictionary,* 41–42. Boston: G. K. Hall, 1977.

Peavy, Charles. *Afro-American Literature and Culture since World War II,* 4. Detroit: Gale Research Co., 1979.

Rush, Theressa Gunnels, Carol Fairbanks Myers, and Esther Spring Arata. *Black American Writers Past and Present: A Biographical and Bibliographical Dictionary,* 1:149–51. Metuchen, N.J.: Scarecrow Press, 1975.

Index

The Author

La Vinia Delois Jennings holds a Ph.D. from the University of North Carolina at Chapel Hill. She is currently an associate professor of English at the University of Tennessee at Knoxville, where she teaches courses in American literature and women's studies. Her publications include articles on Alice Childress and biographical essays on the Harlem Renaissance figures Louise Thompson and Dorothy Peterson.

The Editor

Frank Day is a professor of English at Clemson University. He is the author of *Sir William Empson: An Annotated Bibliography* and *Arthur Koestler: A Guide to Research*. He was a Fulbright Lecturer in American literature in Romania (1980–81) and in Bangladesh (1986–87).